THE 5 PROPERTY MANAGEMENT

A Practical Primer for Managing Residential Properties

KEN DOBLE & COURTNEY WINTERS

THE 5 P'S OF PROPERTY MANAGEMENT

A Practical Primer for Managing Residential Properties

Book formatting and layout design by Saqib_arhsad

Printed in the United States of America

CONTENTS

INTRODUCTION

> *The most serious mistakes are not being made as a result of wrong answers. The truly dangerous thing is asking the wrong questions.*
>
> —PETER DRUCKER
>
> *Great people become great due to the framework, routines and habits they have set for themselves.*
>
> —SUNDAY ADELAJA

The 5 P's of Property Management is a practical process for managing residential properties. While our target audience is those in executive leadership and owners of residential properties, our goal is also for this to be a beneficial reference guide for everyone along the management chain, even including on-site staff such as property managers.

The two authors of this book have a combined forty years of experience managing multifamily apartments. During that time, we have discovered that the residential property business almost universally suffers from a knowledge gap. This gap represents a fundamental disconnect between the site management, on the one hand, and the corporate management, on the other, and can make it difficult for on-site teams to consistently deliver the quality of performance that property owners, as well as corporate-level leaders, expect.

Pooling our experience and our practical knowledge of industry dos, don'ts, and best practices, we aim in this book to close the knowledge gap.

Even though we have found deficiencies on many properties and in many management companies, there are also successfully managed properties all over the United States. We have learned from their example of best practices, and you can too! Few properties are truly unique, and we have yet to encounter a situation calling on us to reinvent the wheel, let alone come up with an alternative to the wheel.

Cataloging and explaining property management on an academic or theoretical level could fill a textbook, perhaps several volumes. This book is a practical guide to making the basics of property management routine, therefore making it easier.

Think of it as a framework for developing your company's own inspection process according to the 5 P's of property management. Each property and each company may have its own specific focus; however, the 5 P's will always be essential in the process of inspecting the property. The checklist has many items, which have been carefully compiled, but each management company or ownership group may have other items missing from this foundational checklist. Use it as a starting point to help you build a 5 P's inspection checklist tailored to *your* property and *your* needs.

Inspection processes may seem simplistic, but they are critical to the overall success of you and your team as well as the management company.

One story that comes to mind is about a manufacturing facility with a very complex system of pipes, valves, and electrical panels that had stopped functioning. Since none of the employees could figure out the problem, the plant manager called in an expert to diagnose the issue. After turning on the system, the expert walked around, listened closely to the sounds of the machinery, and then took a hammer and tapped two times on a section of the pipes, and the problem was solved. He then handed an invoice for $10,000 to the plant manager.

"This is ridiculous!" the plant manager screamed. "I demand an itemized invoice."

The expert handed him an itemized invoice breaking the charges down: $1 for tapping, and $9,999 for knowing where to tap.

Using the 5 P's inspection process will let you know where to tap to fix a problem.

The heart of the *5 P's of Property Management* is the checklist. With these, a property manager, an owner, a management company executive, or all of these, *and* their staff, can tour a property and evaluate it, identifying what is working, what is not working, what needs improvement, who needs help, and who deserves congratulations.

Armed with these checklists and the 5 P's, the reader of this book has the necessary framework to identify, evaluate, think about, and solve the most common problems encountered in property management.

•

You are probably familiar with the 4 P's of marketing. Also known as the *marketing mix*, these are the four key factors involved in marketing any good or service. They include the *product* (the good or service at issue), the *price* (what the consumer pays), the *place* (where the product or service is marketed), and *promotion* (usually, advertising). We have adapted the concepts of the 4 P's of the marketing mix to property management to create the 5 P's of property management: *people, price, product, promotion,* and *process*. Three-fourths of the standard marketing mix—that is, *product, price,* and *promotion*—translates virtually unchanged from classical marketing to modern property management.

In marketing, *product* refers to a good or service that a company offers to customers. Ideally, a product should fulfill a certain consumer demand or be so compelling that consumers believe they need to have it. To be successful, marketers must understand the lifecycle of a product, and managers need to have a plan for dealing with products at every stage of their lifecycle. The type of product also partially dictates how much businesses can charge, where they should place the product, and how they should promote it in the marketplace.

In marketing, *place* is considered separately from *product*, but in property management, *place*—that is, the location of the property—is very much a feature of the product itself. A property is literally inseparable from its location. So we saw no need to separate *place* from *product* when the product in question is a residential property.

Price is the cost consumers pay for a product or service. Marketers must link the price to the product's real and perceived value. They also must consider supply costs, seasonal discounts, and competitors' prices. In some cases, marketers may raise the price to make a product seem more like a luxury item, or lower the price so more consumers will try the product. Marketers also need to determine when and if discounting is appropriate. A discount can sometimes bring in more customers; however, it can also give the impression that a product is less of a luxury item than when it is at a higher price. Also, what good is a sharp increase in revenue triggered by a discount if that discount cuts deeply into the margin of profit? All these basic principles apply to property management as well as marketing in general.

In marketing, *promotion* includes advertising, public relations, and promotional strategy. *Promotion* ties into the other three P's of the marketing mix, as promoting a product shows consumers why they need it and why they should pay a certain price for it. Again, the basic marketing principles of *promotion* apply in property management.

In adapting the 4 P's of marketing to property management, we found it necessary to change *place* for *product* and to add *people* and *process*.

When it comes to property management, we are convinced that *people* is the most critical P among the five. Without your property-management team, what do you really have? And if *people* is the *first* P of property management, *process* is the last. It is, in fact, the final word when it comes to the successful management of a residential property, for *process* describes how you handle everything on your properties, how your customers lease from you and pay you, how you call in work orders, how you pay bills, and on and on.

The 5 P's of property management constitute in themselves a kind of master checklist. When you think about how to manage a property or when you set about evaluating how a particular property is managed, you will find it very useful to think in terms of the five dimensions of *people, price, product, promotion,* and *process*.

Each of these needs to be thought about, planned, examined, properly implemented, and, where necessary, improved upon or repaired. If you can check off all these areas, you can safely conclude that you truly *know* the property in question. If you can honestly conclude that everything pertaining to each of these 5 P's on a given property is operating optimally, you know that you have a successfully managed property. If, however, any P is deficient in any way, you know that you have work to do.

This book will provide you with knowledge of the master checklist (the 5 P's themselves) and a set of action-oriented checklists intended to help you systematically evaluate each P and make decisions about what changes are necessary to make improvements or repairs.

The Authors

Before we turn you loose to read the chapters that follow, we imagine that you have at least one question: Who are we to write a book like this?

Well, let me introduce myself.

I, Ken Doble, have been in the commercial real estate industry for over thirty years and have managed more than forty thousand apartments with over seven hundred employees. I started out as an on-site property manager. I've leased units, cleaned units, and even painted units for turns. I have seen the industry change from paper resident ledger cards and carbon-copy work orders to web-based systems and VR tours.

I promise to freely share with you what I know of best practices, but I invite you even more enthusiastically to learn from my many mistakes and failures because those always taught me so much more than my successes.

With my readers, I also share the good fortune of having Courtney Winters as my coauthor. She is one of the best property managers I have ever worked with or even seen in the business. Originally, I was just going to interview her to include her insights in this book. After speaking with her, however, I knew she would add a wealth of detail and fresh insight as a full-on coauthor. Since starting as a leasing manager in 2015, she has steadily worked her way up through the ranks to where she is at the time of publishing, now working at the corporate level as a regional manager for a student housing management company.

CHAPTER 1

The First P Is for People

The way a team plays as a whole determines its success. You may have the greatest bunch of individual stars in the world, but if they don't play together, the club won't be worth a dime.

—BABE RUTH

When you visit a property, you likely want to know just three things: what's working, what's not, and what needs to be adjusted so that it will work more productively. We will begin with a checklist of eight questions to ask yourself every time you visit a property. Answer these questions satisfactorily, and you are on your way to mastering the first P—*People*!

People are the most important of the 5 P's of property management. In this chapter, you will learn how to find great people and teach them how to become great employees. Follow our guidance, and you will cultivate the right people that you can trust to manage your properties.

PEOPLE CHECKLIST

1. How does the team interact?
2. Is the site fully and adequately staffed?
3. Does the site have any scheduling issues?
4. Are there any performance or personality conflicts on the current team?
5. What team-building events are in place?
6. What are the training plans for the team(s)?
7. Are current performance improvement plans in place and effective?
8. Is communication clear, open, interactive, and effective on every level?

1: How Does the Team Interact?

Sizing It Up

We human beings are biologically fine-tuned to determine the atmosphere of a situation to pick up on potential signs of danger. While we don't typically have to worry about the same types of danger as our prehistoric counterparts did, this evolutionary skill can still be useful when assessing the atmosphere of a team. For example, you can quickly tell that the work setting you are in is healthy because you will see people smiling, an indication that they're lively, alert, and engaged with those around them. However, when something is off balance, you will notice a sense of discomfort because they will appear stressed, like they're walking on eggshells or are restless or distracted.

When your antennas send you an alert, pay attention. Something is likely wrong, although it may take some digging to find out just what the problem or problems may be. *Property management* is first and foremost *people management*. While many personnel issues are visible and obvious, others may reach you only by way of resident complaints, such as unresponsive or shoddy maintenance.

Start with what is in front of you, but also look for the less visible symptoms that indicate the more deeply rooted or systemic problems.

Is employee turnover high? This is typically a sign of leadership problems because a poor or dysfunctional work environment can lead to higher turnover. Bad bosses are at the root of many management issues. People don't often leave good jobs. They leave bad bosses. So assess *management* issues. Is a department understaffed? Do job descriptions align with actual responsibilities? Are hiring practices dysfunctional? Do they result in bringing aboard people unqualified for the positions? Does upper management underappreciate or undervalue employees?

Is competition between employees healthy or toxic? A team requires cohesion and cooperation among its members but also thrives on healthy competition. Leasing competitions, for instance, can raise the productivity of the entire team—unless they begin to foster an unfriendly or toxic environment. An effective property manager monitors the balance between healthy competition and toxic, cutthroat competition, intervening as necessary.

Is tardiness or absenteeism excessive? This could indicate that an employee or employees have issues that impact their roles. Audit attendance and punctuality. An effective manager will detect such unfavorable trends in these two areas and, when needed, talk to the employee about them—in confidence. A good manager looks for any underlying, correctable causes.

Are people taking the appropriate time to recharge? Are they taking lunch breaks? Vacations? This is the other side of the attendance coin. Relentlessly grinding away is as unhealthy and unproductive as making a habit of being late or absent. Downtime is crucial to good performance. If employees routinely work through their lunch breaks, stay late, and are reluctant to take vacation time, you should consider that the workload or other aspects of management are unsustainable. While it is sometimes necessary to work through lunch or stay late, these occasions should be exceptions. When they become the rule, you have a problem to solve. Often, the cause is in the systems—obsolete software that needs updating, leasing processes that need to be re-evaluated. Are additional training programs called for? Is additional staff needed?

Is employee motivation team oriented or fear based? Intimidation can be an effective short-term motivator, but it is unsustainable in the long run. Employees should want to do their jobs well because they care about their careers and understand that their success is tied to the success of the team and the company. If, however, they do their jobs under duress—perpetual fear of reprimand or dismissal—they become desperate. Inevitably, their performance suffers. Motives should be positive, productive, and a matter of mutual satisfaction.

2: Is the Site Fully and Adequately Staffed?

Owners and management companies like to keep their operations lean. That's good management—unless it crosses the line from lean to starved. Depending on the size of a property, the typical staffing categories could include property manager, assistant manager, leasing manager, leasing agents, maintenance supervisor, maintenance technicians, and groundskeepers.

When you assess staffing at a property, begin with the point person, the property manager. That individual's duties and responsibilities impact every aspect of the property operations.

Evaluating a property for the adequacy of its staffing may involve deciding whether to create new positions. Before that, though, you need to ask a more basic question: Does the property have existing positions that are going unfilled? It's very possible that the existence of an open position indicates a problem, especially if it has been open for an extended period of time. To determine whether a problem exists, you should ask the following questions:

- Why is the position open, and how long has it been open?
- Is performance suffering because the position is going unfilled?
- Has the property manager tried to fill the position?
- Is there a shortage of qualified candidates?
- Are screening and hiring policies and procedures adequate at the property?

Hiring

Ken remembers with crystal clarity sitting in a conference room with a candidate for property manager of a troubled 180-unit Class C apartment community in Atlanta. He and his partners had gone through four other property managers, one after another. So they decided to have an all-hands-on-deck effort to interview to find the perfect candidate.

They interviewed several applicants and were not impressed. Finally, a candidate came to the interview on time, professionally dressed—and she even had a written plan for how she was going to turn the site around.

She was the one! They had found their property manager.

She answered all the questions correctly, and everyone cheerfully signed off on her. She took over the site, but in less than a month, she was gone. Terminated.

What happened? She took the job, delegated the duties to the assistant manager, and then made herself completely unavailable to the staff and the residents. The assistant manager was overwhelmed with responsibilities while the property manager stayed behind closed doors.

How could she have fooled a group of experienced property owners into making her an offer? How do you tell the fakes from the real deal?

No one bats a thousand. The lesson here is that sometimes we all make hiring mistakes. So what qualities should you be looking for? Well, that depends on the position.

When hiring a property manager, look for a proven track record. That may be evident in their leadership skills, loyalty within a company, and high energy levels as well as organizational skills. These areas are critical in this position. Also, be sure any employment gaps are satisfactorily explained. Discuss them with the candidate in detail. Become as familiar with their style as possible prior to making them an offer of employment.

When hiring an assistant manager, look for someone who is not only technically proficient but who also has the skills to offer amazing customer service and conflict resolution. Organization and collection skills are givens within the role and should also be among the aspects you are looking for.

When hiring for the leasing staff, look for people who are eager, have great attitudes, and have sales skills—or the ability to learn them. They should also be goal-oriented and motivated. Look for team players with good communication skills who are happy, outgoing, responsible, and capable of handling the office when there are no managers present.

When hiring a maintenance supervisor, you ideally want to promote in-house from your existing maintenance team. Look for someone who is technically sound and proactively communicates with the office staff, the rest of the maintenance team, and the residents. Communication is an integral part of this role, but organizational skills are also important. The maintenance supervisor is responsible for the organization and tracking of vendors' schedules, managing the maintenance team, and keeping up with the shop inventory.

Maintenance technicians and groundskeepers need to be able to communicate well with the maintenance supervisor, the property manager, and residents alike. They need to be able to complete work orders efficiently, correctly, and punctually. Technicians should also maintain a good relationship with vendors so they can fill in for the supervisor when necessary.

All employees should have great integrity, a commitment to teamwork, and respect for their teammates and share in the overall vision for the property.

> *Somebody once said that in looking for people to hire, you look for three qualities: integrity, intelligence, and energy. And if you don't have the first, the other two will kill you. You think about it; it's true. If you hire somebody without [integrity], you really want them to be dumb and lazy.*
>
> —WARREN BUFFETT

Screening

These days, with online hiring sites in plentiful supply, candidates are rarely hard to find. Good candidates, however, are far less plentiful. This is true whether you are a property manager looking for staff, or an owner or upper manager looking to hire a property manager. Interviewing is a time-consuming process, as it should be. Finding the right fit deserves a substantial investment in time and effort. But it is equally important not to waste your time with hit-or-miss interviewing. Create a series of filters to weed out unqualified applicants prior to the interview stage.

Your first filter is the crucial step of putting in the time and effort to write a clear and thorough job description to post, with a full explanation of duties and expectations.

Your second filter is a good screening process for all applications. When you receive a promising résumé, read the résumé critically. Even if a résumé does not show 100 percent of the experience you want but is clear, concise, and persuasive, it is well worth pursuing to the interview level.

Interviewing

Once you have screened an applicant, proceed to scheduling the interview. Resist the temptation to wing it. Always prepare a series of questions. Your questions should encompass issues of personality, character, values, and integrity as well as matters specific to the position.

Unfortunately, it's all too easy when you are in an interview to get caught up in an applicant's personality and neglect some of the more fundamental skills and aptitudes you should be looking for. Courtney has often hired for part-time leasing consultant positions based on personality with the objective of being able to train that employee for administrative competence down the road. That being said, while people can definitely be taught administrative skills, if a candidate is telling you in the interview that they're not very organized or that they have a hard time keeping track of things and multitasking, you may give the person points for honesty but should still recognize that they may not be the best fit.

On the other hand, you don't want to succumb to hiring based exclusively on the perceived urgency of some staffing need at the expense of finding a good fit with your property and your team. It is sometimes better to wait until you have found a great fit with your team than it is to hire somebody just because they are available.

Interviewing:

1. Pay attention to the quality of the answers you get. Are they straightforward and clear, or evasive and obscure?
2. Ask questions that tell you as much about practical experience as they do about stated qualifications. Remember, you are hiring someone who can *apply* knowledge, not someone who *claims to have* knowledge.
3. Ask applicants to tell you stories about their most challenging task, their most successful problem-solving solution, and their biggest mistake (as well as how they dealt with it).
4. Take notes, jotting down the key points and impressions, without, however, diverting your attention from the conversation.

Make it a point to ask three questions as a baseline for any interview:

1. *"What do you feel is the most important skill for somebody in this position?"* Make sure the candidate understands the key skills needed to be successful in this role.
2. *"Tell me about how you handled conflict in your previous position or in your life?"* In property management, conflict is a daily occurrence. The ability to handle it is a necessary part of the job.
3. *"What is the style of management that you most prefer your managers to have?"* This is Courtney's favorite question because it can reveal how applicants understand themselves and what *they* are looking for in the position. It's important to approach an interview with not only the mindset that you're interviewing a candidate to see if they would be a good fit with your team, but also that the candidate is equally interviewing you to decide if your team would be a good fit for them.

Example Questions to Ask When Interviewing a Property Manager Candidate

1. Tell me about your work experience.
2. What traits do you think are most important for hiring a new employee?
3. What are the top three things you like best about being a property manager?
4. What are the top three things you like least about being a property manager?
5. Describe how you lead your teams.
6. Why should we hire you for this job?
7. Describe a situation where you had to fire an employee and why you felt it was needed.

8. Describe a situation where you resolved a team conflict successfully.
9. How do you train your teams?
10. How do you foster a teamwork-based environment?
11. What questions do you have for us?

Tests

Brief tests can also be used as part of the interview, especially for maintenance positions, which require specific technical expertise. For instance, ask maintenance candidates to complete a work order in a vacant or model unit, or have them walk you through how they would complete a work order.

Hiring leasing consultants? Ask them to sell you some specific item. The classic example is to take a pen off your desk, hold it up, and say, "Sell me this pen." In an interview, a test is simply a request that the candidate demonstrates their knowledge and aptitude. If the candidate refuses this demonstration, that's a fairly good indicator that they may not be the right fit for your team.

3: Does the Site Have Any Scheduling Issues?

The property may be fully staffed, but are you appropriately staffing the office during the hours that it's open? Ken had a site that was having trouble leasing. He visited the property on the weekend and found five people waiting for one leasing consultant! When he asked the manager about it, she explained that no one else wanted to work weekends. He was shocked, since the office was open seven days a week.

This was a classic case of hiring without setting appropriate expectations and responsibilities from the beginning. Courtney makes it a point in her job postings and interviews to let applicants know that they will be expected to work evenings and weekends, as there is no point in having adequate staffing if every staff member is only able to work the same hours. You could even make the argument that if you're not able to fully cover your business hours, then your staffing is actually inadequate. Establishing that expectation from the beginning will ensure ease with making the schedule, and that the office is appropriately manned at all times.

4: Are There Any Performance or Personality Issues?

Conflicts on the Current Team?

Common Problems with Teams

Step into almost any organization, and before long, you can sense whether the prevailing culture is positive and productive, a bit off, or downright toxic. At first, the vibe you get may be hard to pin down, but you just *know* something is wrong.

Problems with an organization's culture are caused by problems with the team. The most common include the following:

- **Inadequate training.** There is no shortcut to learning your job. Many personnel problems can be solved by training.
- **Inadequate communication.** Unless leaders and team members can communicate clearly, honestly, and respectfully, they cannot coordinate their efforts effectively. Get people talking with one another. Start by convening team meetings often,

once at the start of the day and briefly at the day's end. As everyone learns to work well with everyone else, it may be possible to have fewer meetings.

- **Insufficient staff.** No matter how good the team is, if the property is chronically short-staffed, important work won't get done or won't get done well, people will burn out, and morale will take a downward dive.

- **A team member is having a personal problem.** The property manager and others should give their teammate all the support they can. The key is empathy, but you also must remember: the job still needs to get done!

- **A team member is failing the team.** If someone habitually fails to pull their weight, it's time for the property manager to challenge them. Assign specific tasks. Require accountability. Wherever possible, use and share objective measures, such as the number of leases signed, the number of work orders completed, and so on.

- **The manager is a micromanager.** Leadership is largely delegation. A poor delegator makes others feel inadequate and powerless, and micromanagers themselves are at risk for burnout.

- **The manager is disorganized.** The best property managers are meticulous. They see the big picture *and* the details, the forest *and* the trees. Disorganized managers are not lost causes; they simply need to be taught how to organize. Organization is a skill that can be taught.

- **The manager is trying to be everyone's friend.** There is nothing wrong with being friendly; however, when leadership is confused with friendship, problems invariably develop. Good leaders are courteous, considerate—and professional to everyone.

- **The manager proves to be a divider instead of a uniter.** Some leaders encourage so much competition within the team that members become backstabbers.
- **The wrong team member is on the team.** Maybe you have a bad apple. Maybe you have a member who resists being a team player. The property manager must make expectations clear, including a commitment to the team. If the maverick member remains an outsider, progressive discipline is called for, and termination may be an option.
- **A team member who lacks integrity, lies, or is grossly incompetent needs immediate attention.** Constructive criticism may help, but progressive discipline is almost certainly necessary. Everybody makes mistakes. Nobody has to lie. A serious lapse in integrity should be a firing offense.

The single biggest problem in communication is the illusion that it has taken place.

—GEORGE BERNARD SHAW

Terminations

When an employee is terminated, it should never come as a surprise. If it does, the failure is as much on you, the manager, as it is on the employee. From the time they apply for a position and every day that they work, employees should know what is expected of them. They should be given the proper instruction and training on how to handle their duties and be offered clear feedback on their performance. If necessary, progressive discipline should be involved, including adequate warnings that failure to correct behavioral or performance issues may well result in termination.

Most terminations are the result of dishonesty, lack of integrity, poor performance, or simply a bad fit with the company team or culture. Some terminations are the direct result of layoffs. These are business decisions that are made through no fault or deficiency of the employee.

5: What Team-Building Events Are in Place?

To work together effectively, the team needs to create a culture of comradery and integrity. Discussion and debate should be encouraged, but once the property manager decides on a course of action, debate stops, and the team must cooperate fully in executing that decision.

Teams do not survive on a mutual commitment to values and missions alone. They are a social group, and the team leader should plan various team events to allow the members to socialize. The leader must see their staff not just as employees but as members of a team that must learn to appreciate, respect, and enjoy one another as teammates and people. As discussed, incentives—especially a bonus system tied to team goals—are crucial to keeping team members both competitive with one another and cohesive as a team.

Great teams are not just assembled. They are built. The team you build depends heavily on the people you hire. But even the best hires need help coming together to make a great team. Upper management and the property manager should collaborate on creating events aimed at building the best team possible.

Group events have been quite successful for Courtney in the past. Throughout her time on-site, she had the opportunity to attend a multitude of activities earned by her team, ranging from escape rooms to murder mystery dinners, trampoline parks, bowling, and even to all-expenses-paid trips to Disney World in years when her team pre-leased all 100 percent of the rooms on their property! Whether it is dining out, horseback riding, hiking, rafting, or group training events, these types of outings have always had a positive impact and helped build great teams.

6: What Are the Training Plans for the Team(s)?

Training is critical to the success of a property. Discuss, review, and evaluate the property manager's program and plans for training new employees. The manager should compile a training binder with material to guide each employee throughout the training process. For example, a leasing agent binder would include a completed sample file. The binder then becomes the property of the employee, who can refer back to it as often as needed.

> *Tell me and I forget, teach me and I may remember, involve me and I learn.*
>
> —BENJAMIN FRANKLIN
>
> *The essence of training is to allow error without consequence.*
>
> —ORSON SCOTT CARD, AMERICAN NOVELIST

Ongoing Training

The great thing about property management is that the profession offers an opportunity for growth. Upper management, as well as the on-site property manager, should be committed to continuous training so that the organization is always developing its human capital. Evaluate the ongoing training and development programs in place at your properties.

Personal improvement training is aimed at acquiring or improving personal skills that employees can apply to property management. A staff member may want to improve their organizational skills, public speaking skills, sales skills, or technical skills. Appropriate training should be made available.

On-the-job training (OJT) is required for almost all new hires. It is not possible to learn everything you need to know from a training binder. The most effective school is often the job itself. Property managers play a central role in mentoring new employees through OJT, not only guiding them but also ensuring the effectiveness and safety of what they do on the job while learning the job. An important note here: new employees should be closely supervised until the manager is comfortable with their knowledge and performance.

Cross-training is important for the continuity of operations. Running a property is a 24/7 operation, and inevitably, there will be times when neither the property manager nor specialized staff will be available. Continuity of operations requires staff members to be cross-trained so that they can pick up the slack in an emergency or when an opportunity presents itself.

In addition to developing training programs, the property manager must draft a cross-training plan to teach the assistant manager (for example) how to do such things as post rents, post accounts payable invoices, administer purchase orders, and so on. All management personnel, whether office staff or maintenance staff, need to know where the water cutoffs are located on the property and how to cut the water off and back on in case of a maintenance emergency. Equally as important is the cross-training program for maintenance. It is imperative that the property manager works with the maintenance supervisor to create an emergency plan and training for the maintenance staff.

Succession Training

Some property managers are reluctant to train their own replacement, but upper management should emphasize succession training as an important on-site responsibility. This may require persuading the incumbent property manager that training a successor poses no threat. On the contrary, it puts the incumbent in a position for a promotion or a bigger role in the company. Teaching has another benefit. It makes the manager a better manager and creates credentials as a trainer. One of the biggest career mistakes property managers make is letting themselves be left behind because they left others behind.

Goals

Leasing and renewal goals. What does every property owner want? The *easy* answer is 100 percent occupancy 100 percent of the time. Unfortunately, it's not usually the *right* answer, which is almost always more complicated. Sometimes, for instance, 95 percent at higher rents is better than 100 percent at lower rents. Most businesses are far too dynamic to be run effectively with static goals. There is no one cookie-cutter prescription for setting property leasing goals, but virtually every property needs to have realistically ambitious goals for lease renewals, leasing velocity (volume of leases your people should be signing weekly, monthly, and annually), prospect visits, and closing ratios. Everyone involved in the property should appreciate the role of social media. Each aspect of media platforms should be reviewed in today's real estate and leasing markets. Owners, property managers, and leasing employees should be fully aligned on strategy, beginning with putting a high priority on monitoring the performance of all social media accounts.

Work Orders and Unit Turn Goals

Work order goals are key to resident renewals. As many residents see it, the number one job of the property manager and leasing staff is to respond promptly and effectively to resident complaints, most of which arise from calls for maintenance to perform work orders. Benchmark performance goals are quantifiable. These goals should be set for the maintenance staff, and they should be accountable for responding to and completing work order requests. Callbacks for maintenance requests are never a good sign.

Unit turn goals should also be a subject of discussion. Property managers, the maintenance teams, and leasing agents should agree on what is expected. It is critically important that strict turn schedules be established and adhered to. Standard turn times should be well established. However, a turn may take longer in a unit that is not vacated in good condition. That possibility should be kept in mind and accounted for when establishing your turn schedule.

Expense Goals

The on-site manager should play a significant role in creating the annual operating budget. Because they oversee expenses on-site and on a daily basis, property managers are in an ideal position to provide owners and top management with a point of view they otherwise do not get. The property managers have the best knowledge of operating expenses and should make it their priority to control expenses in accordance with the budget. Expense goals should also be set accordingly.

Collection Goals

Too often overlooked is setting goals for tracking collections—collections of all accounts, active as well as former resident accounts. Former resident accounts represent potential additional income for the property and should be focused on. This is a great way to increase the overall income at the site.

7: Are Current Performance Improvement Plans in Place and Effective?

Identify and Close Procedure and Execution Gaps

Owners and management companies may put together excellent policies and procedures. However, this does nothing to address gaps that separate procedure from execution. Review the following conversation:

> *Management company regional VP:* "Our people always leave copies of the completed work orders in the units."
>
> *Owner:* "How do you know that?"

VP: "Because it's in the company handbook."

Owner: "You've checked on this—personally? You've seen it happen?"

Regional VP: "I'm no micromanager. The maintenance tech is supposed to do it. It's right there in the handbook."

Seeing this, our bet is that at least some units don't get their copies. We may train them, we may tell them how important this procedure is, and yet we don't have a system in place to confirm the procedure is being done, consistently, as it should be. No matter how skilled a strategist you are, you are only as good as the systems and processes that ensure a seamless transition from policy to action. In the example above, the regional manager should most likely spot-check by calling the resident who requested work in their unit. By doing this, the regional manager can see if the work order was satisfactorily completed and if a copy of the work order was left in the unit. Simply doing this task will most likely ensure that this procedure is being done regularly, as the maintenance team is aware that follow-up is being done.

It is the responsibility of the property manager to close the gap between procedure and execution with on-site monitoring and feedback. Whether the feedback is meant to reinforce positive performance and recognize accomplishments or to identify problems, correct bad habits, and provide guidance for improvement and professional growth, employees need to know where they stand and how they are doing. Moreover, they *want* to know. Look, nobody likes criticism for the sake of criticism, but people need feedback. They want to know how they are performing and how they can perform better. They want to know how they can support the team more effectively.

Management feedback falls into three main categories: *praise, constructive criticism*, and *reprimand*.

Praise

Praise is both easy and pleasant to give. Yet many managers neglect to praise employees.

- They believe: *If it ain't broke, don't fix it.*
- They feel: *I have plenty to do without going out of my way to congratulate an employee just for doing the job they get paid to do!*

Just because these are perfectly understandable attitudes does not mean that they are productive. Reinforce the level of performance you want each employee to deliver by recognizing and praising a job well done. However, praise can also be given too often and too easily. If you high-five your leasing agent for every lease they achieve instead of simply acknowledging that they are one step closer to their goal, you might be sending the wrong message. Set milestone goals and praise employees along the way. Praise should be given, but it should be attached to milestone achievements. The more specific the praise, the more effective the reinforcement.

Praise should not be given for expectations. Expect great customer service, taking the initiative on a project, and even completing an assortment of assigned tasks on time and without error. Inspect what is expected and discuss your expectations often.

Constructive Criticism

Constructive criticism is positive management feedback intended to improve performance and should always have the intention of creating an effective change. Constructive criticism does not scold, blame, humiliate, or punish. It is a means for employees to learn from an error or a deficiency in performance. They can then focus on doing better the next time. Constructive criticism should be used to empower the employee. It should not only encourage the employee to do better but also it will help them develop their career.

Constructive criticism should be positive and should help the *employee* achieve the level of performance *you* expect.

A good way to ensure that your *criticism* is truly constructive is to sandwich it between two pieces of *praise*. The praise must be legitimate and warranted. So do your best to recognize something positive to create a receptive context in which you can express your criticism. For instance:

> Fred, you have been a real asset to the maintenance team since you joined us last month. Residents appreciate your caring personality and your efficiency.
>
> I did get a comment from one the other day, however, pointing out that you left the old hardware behind when you replaced the wall switch in 3B. I'm not saying the resident was angry, but she did go out of her way to tell me that she had to clean this up herself. I understand you want to be in and out of a service call quickly. I appreciate that. But take a moment for a last look and make sure you've cleaned up after yourself.
>
> That said, keep up the great work!

The *sandwich* recipe is simple: **praise-criticism-praise.**

Reprimand

Sometimes constructive criticism is not enough. Reprimands must be made immediately when an employee violates or neglects stated responsibilities or work rules. In addition, if an employee is behaving in an unacceptable manner, then reprimanding the employee is warranted.

Disrespecting another employee, whether they are the supervisor, peer, or subordinate, and showing discourtesy to a resident are examples of employee transgressions that must be addressed immediately with a reprimand.

Understand that the goal of a reprimand is to advise the employee that the behavior in question is unacceptable and must not be repeated. Reprimands need to be delivered calmly and in a professional manner. Clearly explain the nature of the transgression and why it is unacceptable. Establish what needs to be done to remedy the behavior or incident and how to avoid repetition. Collaborate with the employee and inform them of the course of action that must be taken to remedy the situation.

Once the reprimand is complete, ask the employee three questions:

1. "Do you understand why what you did is unacceptable?"
2. "Do you understand what you need to do?"
3. "Do you agree with that solution?"

It is important to note that reprimands should always be made privately and never publicly, as this may create shame, anger, and/or resentment. Public reprimands cause harm both to the employee who is being reprimanded and to the team alike.

If the behavior is serious enough to warrant possible dismissal, the reprimand should be made both in person and in writing, spelling out the infraction and the conditions under which the employee will be terminated.

Incentives

Incentives can be either positive or negative. Any behavioral scientist will attest that positive incentives typically produce more successful and durable results. Negative incentives are sometimes appropriate responses to discourage or prevent unacceptable behavior and actions.

Positive incentives

Praise, including celebrating achievements, is not only a useful positive incentive but also builds team cohesion and morale. Praise should be public and delivered in the presence of other team members. Gathering the team together for a lunch break or to share a celebratory cake or other treat is a pleasant way to recognize excellent performance and other achievements.

Tokens, such as lapel pins, mugs, movie or sports tickets, and so on, can be used to recognize various milestones or the achievement of certain set goals. These may be distributed at team meetings.

The most obvious incentive is, of course, **money**. It speaks every language, including the language of business. It also speaks of value delivered and a job well done. Yet, over the years, numerous studies have shown that money is not invariably the silver bullet among incentives. Based on a survey by the respected Boston Consulting Group, ten factors are the top creators of employee happiness:

1. Appreciation for work

2. Good relationships with colleagues
3. Good work-life balance
4. Good relationships with superiors
5. Company's financial stability
6. Learning and career development
7. Job security
8. **Attractive fixed salary**
9. Interesting job content
10. Company values

Note that salary is number 8 out of the ten. The whole point of mentioning this survey is to highlight the fact that there are many other ways than monetary bonuses to motivate your staff.

Face it, salary and other compensation measured in money are important. Costly? Yes. But how costly is it to lose your most valuable employees? This said, there are many powerful incentives that cost relatively little or nothing at all and can be introduced at any property.

Are any of these incentives used regularly on the property?

Do managers and supervisors say thank you?
Verbal thank-yous should be commonplace throughout the workday. A handwritten note or perhaps a gift card is an effective way to acknowledge special performance.

Are managers and supervisors on a first-name basis with employees?
Using the employee's first name in many interactions acknowledges that person *as* a person.

Are high-performing employees honored publicly?

Publicly honor top performance weekly or monthly. Create a Wall of Fame.

Do employees have good equipment?
Everyone appreciates an efficient desk, a comfortable chair, and an up-to-date computer. Maintenance staff needs top-notch tools and equipment. Make every job as comfortable, efficient, and safe as possible.

Does the office celebrate together?
Recognize birthdays, work anniversaries, project comple-tions, and team milestones with a celebration, even if just a pizza party or a cake.

Does the office give gifts?
Everyone appreciates coupons and gift cards.

Does management recognize employees as more than em-ployees?
Consider supporting employees involved in charitable or-ganizations, athletic competitions, and the like by giving them access to physical or online bulletin boards. Let them share what is meaningful to them.

Is positivity reinforced?
Managers and supervisors should foster a positive environ-ment by accenting good things, uplifting things, and acts of kindness and courtesy. Call these out at routine staff meet-ings.

Is community service encouraged?

Consider giving employees paid days to be used to serve the community. Encourage their involvement in organizations that are important to them.

With respect to incentive and compensation packages, upper management should assess the following in the context of competing employers:

- Health care
- Retirement
- Paid time off
- Workplace flexibility
- Wellness program
- Tuition reimbursement
- Flexible and family-friendly schedules
- Pay raises
- Performance bonus policy
- Life insurance
- Professional development and training

If upper management discovers overall compensation and benefits are not competitive, and you are having a hard time filling open positions, you may need to consider modifying these to become competitive in the marketplace.

Use positive performance incentives strategically

In property management, commissions paid for signing leases are well-established as incentives. Property managers can build on the established concept by creating different types of incentive packages, for instance, a competition among the staff for who can achieve the most social media reviews that specifically mention them, the most renewals, and so on. Obviously, the competition must span a specific period of time. In most cases, a month works best. It is long enough to get results, but not so long that everyone loses interest. To avoid throwing money away or devaluing the prize, set a team or group minimum for anyone to qualify. Minimum standards incentivize the performance of the entire team.

Again, simply throwing money at any goal is not a strategy. Ensure that your incentive plan rewards the things your marketing strategy requires. Ken once talked to the leasing team at a 572-unit community in Dallas. They complained that prospects avoided leasing the upstairs units because nobody wanted to walk up the stairs.

"Okay," he told them. "I'm taking the manager to lunch. Anyone who leases an upstairs unit today will get a double leasing commission."

By the time Ken came back from lunch, team members had leased four upstairs units. The right incentive, targeting what *you* need, is powerful. The right incentive creates belief where only doubt existed before. Before the incentive, the leasing team viewed upstairs apartments as worthless. After the incentive, they became prizes.

Strategically Evaluating a Property's Incentive Plan

1. Be certain your property's incentive plan rewards the right things.
2. Determine how competitive your bonus and commission plans are.

- An owner or management company that pays $10 per lease when competitors pay $75 will have a hard time attracting and retaining the best leasing staff. You could pay a higher base salary, but then you will diminish the incentive of high commissions.

3. Sell the value of your commission plan to your employees.

- Talk to the team.
- Ask the team if they understand the bonus plan.
- Make certain team members understand that their additional compensation is directly related to their performance.

4. Make your monetary incentives simple.

- The simplest propositions usually strike employees as the fairest and most generous.

5. Set ambitiously realistic goals.

- If incentives are tied to impossible objectives, healthy employee competition will quickly turn to frustration, which is incredibly demotivating.

8: Is Communication Clear, Open, Interactive, and Effective on Every Level?

Effective communication across the team, between the property manager and upper management, and between staff and residents is essential to efficient property management. Assess the quality of communication at the property by asking these questions:

Communication Checklist

1. Are communications simple, direct, and clear?
2. Are instructions and directives accompanied by an explanation of *why* the assignment needs to be done and why it may be critical to the goals of the property?

3. Are employees told why an assignment must be completed on time?
4. Are communications interactive with dialogue?
5. Is everyone on the team given a voice?
6. Are all questions being encouraged?

Summary

Every business is a people business, but none more than property management. When you make a site visit, focus first on people issues. Start by opening yourself to the feel of the place. Take note of the emotional climate in the office. If it feels off, pay closer attention and dig a little deeper. While handling personal conflict can be intimidating, it helps to remember that most problems do have a solution.

Beyond what you feel about the property and its staff, look at the basics. Is the property adequately staffed? Are there open positions—especially positions that have been open for a long time? Examine work schedules. Look for conflicts and deficiencies in them. And while you are focused on possible conflict, determine if the management team is burdened by any performance or personality conflicts.

Remember that you are looking at a *team*. No team happens by accident. Ensure that the property manager has put team-building events in place and has a sound set of training plans in operation. Examine performance and focus on improvement. These will require planning, so talk about improvement plans on-site.

From the perspective of overall management, consider the need for changes in incentive plans when the property is not performing as expected.

Above all, people are the most important part of the 5 P's, which is why we chose to focus on this topic first.

CHAPTER 2
The Second P Is for Pricing

> *The single most important decision in evaluating a business is pricing power ... If you've got the power to raise prices without losing business to a competitor, you've got a very good business. And if you have to have a prayer session before raising the price by 10 percent, then you've got a terrible business.*
>
> —WARREN BUFFETT
>
> *Perhaps the reason price is all your customers care about is because you haven't given them anything else to care about.*
>
> —SETH GODIN

It is important to remember that *price* is key. However, potential residents mainly consider four criteria when they are looking for a new apartment:

1. **Location:** The community must be practical and convenient with easy access to work, schools, places of worship, transportation, and other amenities of importance to prospective residents.

2. **Price:** Once prospects have identified their desired location, they decide if the price range is within their budget.

3. **Property-specific features:** The important features of a property include the number of rooms, baths, square footage, pet policy, parking spaces, appliances, on-site amenities, and so on.

4. **Staff:** A property may have the right location and price as well as other attractive features, but if the on-site staff is rude or otherwise unhelpful, the potential resident will likely lease from one of your competitors. If your staff is rude, unfriendly, incompetent, or unresponsive, simply multiply factors 1 through 3 by 0, because they likely won't matter anymore. Nobody wants to live where they feel unwelcome and even unwanted.

When it comes to deciding on a home, *location* and *price* are the most critical points. The property *must* have a practical and convenient location, and the property *must* have an affordable price. While absolute, these typically exist within a range of tolerance and are at least somewhat flexible. A prospect may be willing to make certain compromise tradeoffs between *location* and *price*, for instance, or between proximity to desirable stores and restaurants versus a shorter work commute. But the range is always limited by reality. Moreover, factor #1, *location*, is built into the ground. The location of the property is what it is—a given.

Of the four factors, #2, *price*, can be analyzed and potentially changed most quickly to boost leasing.

Factor # 3, *property-specific features*, may have some flexibility in the long run. Some amenities can be added or upgraded; however, prospects typically base their decision on current amenities.

Factor #4, *staff*, is the easiest to address and adjust. Additional training may be required or a change in staffing may be necessary.

How important is pricing? It is not just a piece of the pie, it is the whole pie! One of the most important things a property manager does is *increase* prices, and therefore revenue, for the apartments, which includes rents, fees charged, utility chargebacks, and so on.

The question is, how do you set the *right* price? Begin with the following checklist:

PRICING CHECKLIST

1. Have you reviewed your property's pricing matrix?
2. Have you reviewed other income?
3. Have you reviewed the competitive market surveys?
4. Have you reviewed and adjusted specials and renewals accordingly?

1: Review Your Property's Pricing Matrix

Pricing almost any product is rarely a set-it-and-forget-it process. Markets are dynamic, which means that it is important not only to monitor conditions and adjust prices accordingly but also to check your property's pricing matrix at least weekly.

Some property-management companies use revenue management software to evaluate and adjust their prices automatically.

Reports to Review Often

One basic tenet of management is the frequent reviewing of reports pulled that reflect your property's performance. Your property should generate updated versions of the following reports, which you should review prior to evaluating your pricing:

- **Updated market survey:** This should be broken down by such details as unit mixes, specials, utilities, move-in fees, deposits, and so on.
- **Unit availability report:** This report shows which floorplans have the most notices to vacate or the biggest vacancy, so you can check your pricing by unit type. This report also shows which units have been vacant the longest.
- **Leasing report:** This tells you what units and floorplans are leasing the best.
- **Current pricing/hot sheet:** This is a current listing of pricing for each unit on the property, including specials, used mainly by the leasing team.

Laser in on Floorplans and Availability

The property's **floorplans** and **unit availability report** deserve special attention. They highlight the vital signs in the life of the site. The first report shows notices to vacate, current vacant units, and related information, and the second report tells you which units have been vacant the longest.

When interpreting floorplans and availability reports, these are the most important things you should be looking for:

- **Current and future supply of units.** Is your supply excessive? Look for patterns. Determine the cause. Does the property have a large number of lease expirations in certain months compared to others? Does the property suffer from a large number of skips or evictions?

- **Notably slow-leasing and fast-leasing units and/or floor-plans.** Again, look for patterns. You want to determine which units and/or floorplans are leasing slower than others and, conversely, which ones move notably faster. You should expect to have harder-to-lease units. For example, a unit that is on the basement or terrace level may be much harder to lease than a walk-in-level unit, provided that the rents are equal. Such units are obvious candidates for price adjustments to reflect their location relative to other units on the sites. If certain units or floorplans are leasing at a notably rapid rate, figure out what factors and features are driving that activity. Look at the location and amenities. Offer special leasing incentives on the hardest units to lease. Do not offer blanket specials on all units without reviewing leasing reports first. Also, consider the highest performing units—does their popularity offer a solid opportunity for increasing the price on these units or floorplans?
- **Down units or expensive turns.** These reports will bring to light down units that may be hidden at the site. Units that sit for days and weeks on the availability report should be flagged for a walk-through. You need to determine what is causing the units to sit idle for so long. Talk to the maintenance supervisor. Is there a shortage of turn crews? Or does the condition of the unit require major cleaning or repairs? These issues can make for expensive turns; therefore, the property manager may be reluctant to note that on the books.
- **If the site's marketing program and specials are focused on both current *and* future supply.** Don't run yesterday's specials today. Specials serve two functions. First, they give

prospects a reason to come to you instead of going to your competition. Second, they boost slow-moving floorplans. Supply and demand are in a dynamic relationship. You cannot successfully run yesterday's specials today unless you are certain they are satisfying a need that still exists.

It seems a no-brainer, but we can't tell you how many times we have reviewed a property's availability reports and then reviewed the property's ads and marketing only to discover that they were running specials on floorplans that formerly had a vacancy issue but are now doing just fine. Always check currently reported availability against current marketing campaigns and specials.

Leasing Velocity

Leasing velocity is to your property what a speedometer is to a driver. It lets you know how quickly or how slowly you are leasing units. Leasing velocity feedback is relative to what the competition is doing. For example, if leasing has changed to more or less than you normally have on the property, you need to understand why. Knowing what the leasing velocity is will help you determine the correct pricing.

2: Review Other Income

Amenity-Based Pricing

Amenity-based pricing is pricing that charges for unit-specific items such as fireplaces, views, higher floors, locations within the property, floorplan sizes, closet space, and so on.

The idea is to look at all your units and determine what amenities are more desirable for the residents and what premiums they are willing to pay for them. Individual upcharges need to be competitive. Even modest monthly upcharges add up fast and can really drive a property's income. Many of the best property-management software packages include special ways to track amenity-based pricing.

Creating different floorplan mixes gives prospective residents choices, and choice is something virtually all consumers value. If there is a downside to providing a range of choices, it is the risk of confusing prospects and leasing agents with too many options. Keep it simple, but make the differences distinctive.

Upgrade-Based Pricing

In the real estate world, upgrade-based pricing is often called a *value-added business model*. Typical value adds include upgraded kitchens, bathrooms, flooring, and so on. This calls for investments that justify—both to prospective residents and to property owners and managers—the costs of the upgrades. For instance, if upgrading appliances costs $1,100 per unit and you can get $25 more in rent each month, your annual return on the added costs would be 27 percent.

Doing the basic math is simple. (Amount of annual rental increase/Cost of upgrades) Just take the annual rental increase and divide it by the cost to install the upgraded appliances. But figuring out which upgrades will pay the highest possible returns requires that you start shopping your comps. You need to understand what the competition is offering and then determine what you can productively upgrade in your units.

We have sometimes hedged our bets by regularly updating model units with color changes, countertop and appliance replacements, lighting upgrades, and the like. Show prospects both an upgraded unit and the base unit that is available. Let *them* decide. It is always easier to sell customers on their own ideas than it is to persuade them to buy yours. Having choices gives the potential resident options.

Many apartment companies install the upgrades only on turnover of the unit; however, it is also possible to do a limited amount of work on occupied units at lease renewal. We have upgraded appliances, countertops, cabinet doors, light fixtures, toilets, and faucets in occupied units without creating too much disruption.

Upgrade-based pricing is one of the fastest ways to increase the value of a property, but it can be difficult to execute an upgrade program without a capital funding event such as a refinance or owner funding to pay for the improvements.

Pets Don't Live for Free

One of the quickest ways you can drive revenue is to do a pet audit on-site. Most properties charge a pet fee or even a monthly pet rent, often on a per-pet basis. Pet charges may be viewed as a practical necessity to cover the costs of the likely damage pets inflict on flooring, doors, window screens, window blinds, and so on.

How many times have you walked a property and seen more pets living on your property than you remember? When your team does their quarterly inspections, they should be checking for unauthorized pets. We often hear the excuse that Fido is only "staying for a few days," but unenforced rules are useless. Moreover, free-rider pet residents are unfair to those residents who are paying their fair share for their four-legged companions.

Enforcing the rules and collecting the deposit or rent does not require the staff to become unpleasant. Consider providing pet owners with stickers to be placed on doors, so that maintenance or management teams do not accidentally let a pet out when they must enter the unit for maintenance requests or inspections. Also, the stickers alert firefighters to the presence of pets. Pet owners appreciate that—and offering the stickers is a non-confrontational way to get the residents themselves to let you know if they have pets in their units. We have seen pet audits increase a site's pet-rental income by 500 percent or more. It's really an easy way to add income to the site.

Accepting Pets Can Be a Unique Selling Proposition

Pet rent and pet audits can get your property significant additional income, but you may be able to gain an even more strategic advantage from accepting pets. Your team's market survey should include what surrounding comps charge for pets as well as which competitors allow them and which do not. Based on the result of the survey, you may find that allowing pets provides you with a very significant marketing advantage, especially if any of your competitors do not allow pets. We have seen properties lease more quickly by accepting pets. Consider going the extra mile and creating a dog park on the property. This is certainly a nice benefit for the dogs, and pet-owning residents also appreciate the opportunity to socialize with other animal lovers. At one of Courtney's properties, several of her residents even created a dog park GroupMe where all the dog owners coordinated among themselves for trips to the park and doggy birthday parties. Something this small and low effort can have a huge impact on creating a feeling of community among your residents and increase resident retention.

3: Review Competitive Market Surveys

To price accurately and productively, you need to know what the competition is asking and offering. Pricing is always relative to the marketplace.

Where Does Your Property Fit In? Determine Your Bracket Position

Every property has a rental bracket relative to its competitors. You need to find out where you fit within the bracket defined by comparable properties. For instance, if your property is new—say, two or three years old—and is in a perfect location with outstanding floorplans, you likely are at or near the top of your bracket. This means your property should set rents at the top of the market.

The pricing bracket is a straightforward concept, but you need to be aware of extraneous issues that can impact your pricing power regardless of where you are within the bracket. For instance, if a major employer near your property has suddenly laid people off, the entire market may suffer. If, on the other hand, some new major employer has appeared on the scene, you may find yourself in the enviable situation of enjoying increased demand for housing. That should start you thinking about pricing higher than your accustomed bracket. Situational awareness is critical.

Know where your property stands in its pricing bracket. These days, revenue management pricing system software is common. These applications can be enormously useful, but they can also make you lazy. While the software is good at calculation, the program is only as good as the data you feed into it. Make certain your information is accurate and that you are using the right brackets for determining your competition and setting your prices. Time and again, we have seen the consequences of picking the wrong comps. This is a common error when a new owner acquires a property or when a management company assumes a new asset. Select the wrong comps, and you will either undercut the rents or overstate them and have trouble leasing.

Sometimes, in the process of an acquisition, the buyer will show prospective investors or underwriters a proforma based on a selection of comps skewed to the upper range of the bracket. This allows the buyer to project rental revenue that may well be inflated. Doing this deliberately is a major gamble. If the market has a low supply with few deals coming online, you likely will be successful and your owners will be happy. On the other hand, you could easily end up with a property in which actual rents are way lower than what was projected to investors or owners. If you try to keep rents high in relation to the property's more similar comps, you will see slower leasing and higher turnover at the property.

The objective of pricing is to be neither too high nor too low but just right. This requires applying good judgment to accurate data, thereby finding the most advantageous position within the correct bracket. That said, the most common error is not pricing too high but pricing too low. We caution managers never to confuse low pricing with effective marketing and leasing. Anyone can lease an apartment for a dollar, and many do—for a time. But lowballing is not a sustainable strategy or business model. If you find that you rely on low rental pricing as your only difference in the marketplace, you need to find some other features to promote.

The pricing bracket should help keep you from overshooting or undershooting your pricing. You still must take into account the current marketplace conditions that impact the demand for your product. You also need to ensure that you are using correct, timely,

and accurate data to determine the proper pricing brackets. Don't cal-
culate the bracket based exclusively on rental income; include other
income as well. For instance, do your comps charge deposits? Are their
fees non-refundable? What do they charge in storage fees? Leave no
stone unturned and ignore nothing. Your job is to maximize income
from the property. This is achieved mainly through pricing and occupancy, but it also requires that you never leave money on the table.

Market Surveys

All market surveys are not created equal.

First, a useful market survey must contain the right information.
Ensure that your market comps contain at least these items:

1. Property name
2. Property address
3. Unit counts and types
4. Square footage of floorplan types
5. Price for each floorplan
6. Specials
7. Effective price
8. Utilities included and excluded
9. Upfront fees and security deposits
10. Amenities

    a.   In-unit washer and dryer
    b.   Washer and dryer connections
    c.   All utilities included
    d.   Balcony
    e.   Fitness center
    f.   Business center

g. Pool

h. Pet area/dog park

i. Volleyball court

j. Basketball court

k. Carwash

l. Storage units

11. Occupancy and pre-leased information
12. Pet fees and policy
13. Date of the survey
14. Person updating the shopping report

Next, a market survey should be consistently updated. Some companies require them to be updated monthly, while others call for weekly updates. In our experience, weekly updates are best. This is the most effective way to find out if your competitors are doing something to which you need to respond.

Always cross-check pricing data from Apartments.com, RentPath, Craigslist, Instagram, your competitors' websites, and so on to ensure that your market survey data is accurate. Sometimes, your leasing agents will call the competition, who may—or may not—tell your team the correct pricing or occupancy. You need other sources to corroborate and confirm the data you collect so that your pricing decisions can be made correctly. Keep in mind that many communities are on a revenue management system with prices changing continually. Data is only accurate for short periods since communities frequently adjust their prices. Whenever leasing slows, update your market surveys and address changes in pricing accordingly.

Leasing Cliff Dives

*Something was very wrong. Ken had a 212-unit apartment community in Atlanta with a great property manager and regional manager. They had done everything right in terms of market survey research. But suddenly the projected occupancy was dropping—fast. The leasing had all but stopped! Had the property taken a **leasing cliff dive**?*

When performance varies unexpectedly and without obvious explanation, you must act fast to find out what is happening. Ken drove out to the property and started asking questions related to the 5 P's. The property had a good leasing team, great product, and, per the market survey, was competitive with the surrounding properties.

They seemed to be doing everything right. So what was causing this sharp drop-off in leasing activity?

Ken asked the leasing agent to call back some of the prospect traffic and see if she could find out where these people had leased. It takes effort to track prospects down, but you will find that most people want to be helpful. After connecting with several of the prospects who had toured the community, the leasing agent had an answer that explained what was going on in the submarket.

A competing property had just finished a massive and attractive renovation and was now leasing fast. They promoted their investment by doing a look-and-lease special, offering two months free if the prospect leased that day. The special was not advertised but offered only in person when a prospect visited the property. So when leasing agents called the property for a market survey, they were not told about the look-and-lease special.

Pricing reports are only as good as the information that goes into them. The lesson learned here was that whenever leasing is tanking for no apparent reason, use the onion approach, taking the time to peel back *all* layers until the core is revealed.

We use different services and methods to confirm the pricing reported to our sites. CoStar and Axiometrics are great services for getting confirmation of competitor pricing. A cheaper way is to follow your competitors on Apartments.com, Craigslist, Instagram, and other online marketing sources. Doing this should keep you informed of any major specials—provided they are not in-person exclusives. Secret shopping services can be utilized when you suspect that your competitors are withholding information about their specials.

4: Review Specials and Renewals

Review Your Current Specials

Do you know the French word for *real estate*? It is *l'immobiliers*, which means, literally, "the immovables." Clearly, French property owners and managers never need to be reminded that they are in the business of selling—or leasing—the immovable. *Location*, the number one factor in a prospective resident's leasing decision, is a given. It is a factor over which you have no control. Fortunately, the number two factor, *price*, is very much within your power to adjust and tweak—in a word, to manage.

Sometimes prices need to be raised or lowered generally throughout the property. More often, however, owners, management companies, and property managers use specials to draw traffic to their property, set the property apart from the offerings of competitors, review slow-moving units and floorplans, and encourage renewals. Specials, therefore, should always appear *special*—out of the ordinary and not to be missed.

Whenever you visit a property, review its current specials. First, what kinds of specials are in use at the property? In the business of residential leasing, specials become *common* precisely because they are proven to work. Here are the most common leasing specials used:

- **Free rent.** This is *the* classic leasing special. Some markets give away a half month to two months' rent free at move-in. This works in some markets, as long as your product is competitive; however, it is not used very much in the higher end of the rental market. In certain markets, specials like this may be interpreted as red flags signaling something wrong with the apartment. Know what your market is looking for.
- **Gift cards.** We all know this is just a different form of free rent; however, it is coded to marketing costs instead of rental concessions. A prospect is less likely to interpret it as a red flag. Gift cards are common on new construction lease-ups.
- **Raffle or drawing for prizes.** This works great! We have seen this work with AirPods, iPads, laptops, and vacation trips. Adding second- and third-place prizes are a good idea, too. Primed with prizes of real value, this is a great way to create a marketing buzz for your community. Instagram, Craigslist, and other media advertising should be used to enhance the buzz from the drawing. **Consult your legal advisor about state and local laws applicable to all types of drawings or games**.
- **Games of chance or skill.** Create games to generate excitement. Use something like "spin the wheel" or "throw the dart" to reveal available prizes. Games can be used for new move-ins as well as renewals. **Again, consult your legal advisor about**

state and local laws applicable to all types of drawings or games.

- **Free merchandise or trips.** Some companies purchase cruise packages to give away once a lease is signed at move-in. Other incentives work just as well, depending on your market. At one of our student-housing communities, we had prospects really get excited about Apple HomePods. Everyone loves getting freebies, provided they have some genuine value. One of Courtney's properties ran a hugely popular "Rentmas" leasing special for their next lease term, advertising a different giveaway each day for twelve straight days. It is designed to create a sense of urgency. There's a limit on how many people can sign up each day. For example, the special would be for the first twenty people who signed up that day. Each item typically ranged anywhere from $50 to $150, and the selection changed each year based on what was popular at the time. Even something small like this can generate a huge amount of buzz, and they often had a waitlist of leases to send out once they got to each specific day.

Review Your Pricing Policy on Renewals

Any review of pricing at a property must include consideration of the difference between pricing lease renewals versus pricing new leases. Many companies price renewals lower than new leases because they understand that it is cheaper to keep a resident in place than have them vacate and then turn the unit. The complete turnkey of a unit can be expensive. Consider the impact on your property's performance:

- Rental losses during vacancy
- Marketing costs to find new residents

- Time and money cost to screen prospective residents
- Leasing incentives to employees
- Maintenance costs
- Capital improvements required to make the unit competitive
- Cleaning and painting
- Utilities—some utilities must be kept on even when a unit is vacant

These costs add up, so it is very important to carefully review with the property manager the site's turnover rate. The formula for calculating the rate is simple. If you have one hundred units rented at an apartment complex and fifty move-outs for the year, the turnover ratio is 50 percent (50 residents that moved/100 total residents for year = 0.5; 0.5 x 100 = 50%). According to the National Apartment Association (NAA) Survey, the average garden-style apartment turnover ratio was 51 percent in 2018.

There is the more intangible value of retaining a renewal resident. Not only does this save you the cost of screening new applicants, but there is also a significant comfort level in doing business with a resident who is a known quantity.

5: Do You Need a Revenue Management System?

I think what makes AI different from other technologies is that it's going to bring humans and machines closer together. AI is sometimes incorrectly framed as machines replacing humans. It's not about machines replacing humans, but machines augmenting humans. Humans and machines have different relative strengths and weaknesses, and it's about the combination of these two that will allow human intents and business process to scale 10x, 100x, and beyond that in the coming years.

—ROBIN BORDOLI

The argument for using revenue management software to guide pricing strategy is compelling, especially if you take the time to understand that the effective revenue management of a property is more complex than simply shooting for maximum occupancy all the time. The more productive objective is to price optimally—that is, to price in ways that don't just yield the maximum demand but also ensure that the demand carries with it the highest possible revenue value.

This is nearly impossible to do by the seat of your pants. You must measure what economists call *price elasticity*, the consumer's willingness to pay. Put simply, consumers cannot be forced to pay more than what they believe is appropriate. In commodity businesses, finding the right price points can be done effectively by trial and error. You set a price, see what happens, see what your competition is doing, and adjust and readjust accordingly. In real estate, however, adjusting price is like turning an aircraft carrier around. It cannot be done on a dime. Each lease sticks you with a pricing decision that is most likely for the lease term of at least one year.

To accurately model elasticity in your market, you need detailed, historical market data, including rents, occupancies, and the new units coming online. There are many variables when it comes to pricing, among them floorplans, market comp pricing, and occupancies. Pricing is not easy for anyone to do. Computer programs make it simpler to accomplish this task with fewer errors.

Advantages of Revenue Management System

The most compelling single advantage of using a good revenue management system is that it can often increase the total revenue of a site by a larger range than the cost of the software. In other words, it will pay for itself. Other advantages of revenue management systems include the following:

a. Systematizes the approach to pricing, which allows owners and management companies greater control and visibility on pricing at the sites.

b. Reduces resistance to increasing pricing aggressively on long-time residents at renewals. It is human nature not to be as objective about renewal pricing when management allows personal relationships with residents to override sound financial judgment.

c. Pricing systems react faster than humans to shifting market conditions. If you have a lot of two bedrooms coming up on the availability report, the software will push down pricing immediately. The manual (human) process of pricing properties is not nearly as fast.

d. Is proactive rather than reactive. When it comes to market competitor-focus factors versus internal-focus factors (such as availability, leasing traffic, renewal velocity, and so on), revenue management systems do a much better job of proactively focusing on your internal factors rather than simply reacting to competitor price changes.

e. Increases income. Revenue management software is cost-effective; however, take note that the claims of many software vendors vary widely. Most vendors promise anywhere from a 2 percent to a 7 percent increase in income.

My generation grew up worshipping the occupancy gods. We learned that if you were not 95 percent-plus occupied, the asset was failing. But that's not necessarily true anymore.

—David Hannan, senior vice president at the Morgan Group, a Houston-based developer, commenting on how revenue management software grew revenue 5 percent above expectations, increasing overall revenue generated from his company's property, whether it was fully occupied or not.

The Downside of Using Revenue Management Software

Revenue management systems are not without drawbacks. We have reviewed the *pros*; here are the major *cons*:

- The software can be expensive, with costs (depending on the vendor) running between $15 and $24 per unit per year at the time of this writing, in addition to initial setup fees. It is certain these costs will drop over time as such software becomes more commonplace.
- Your staff could be resistant to rolling out and using these comprehensive types of software systems, which they may see as a form of automation threatening their jobs or, at the very least, limiting their control and creative latitude within their jobs.
- The market/revenue management pricing software problem: Once you adopt revenue management software, you no longer know what income increases your property would have achieved *without* the system. If a company says their product

increases the income on a site by 2 percent on average, and they are testing in markets that are going up by 2 percent, did they really add any value?

Revenue management software: the major vendors at the time of writing

- RealPage offers YieldStar, which promises to "outperform the market by 2 percent to 7 percent."
- Yardi offers RENTmaximizer, which cites users who experienced "7.37 percent rent growth, beating respective markets by 3.25 percent."
- Grande Central offers RentPush, which includes case studies of properties with 9 percent to 15 percent annual increases in actual occupied rent.

In the end, discussing the pros and cons of revenue management software may be rendered moot by the future itself. Currently, virtually all properties use some form of property-management software. We believe that all future iterations of such software will have revenue management components built in. Sooner or later, therefore, we will all be using some type of full-featured revenue management software.

Summary

Remember, pricing is not just a piece of the pie. It is the whole pie! When it comes to expenses and income, it all comes out of the same revenue pie.

Location and price are the two primary drivers of a prospect's decision to lease or not lease at a given property. Owners and managers cannot change the property's location, but they can change the price of a lease. While the first instinct is to lower the rent, one of the most important things a property manager does is *increase* prices for the apartments, including rents, fees charged, utility charge-backs, and so on. The real question is not whether the price is low enough or high enough, but if it is even the right price. Determine this by reviewing the Pricing Checklist provided in this chapter.

CHAPTER 3
The Third P Is for Product

You never get a second chance to make a first impression.

—ANDREW GRANT

When the product is right, you don't have to be a great marketer.

—LEE IACOCCA

If you want to sell something, you need to have a compelling *product*, the third of the 5 P's. We know that the two variables of location and price are, from the standpoint of the consumer, very nearly non-negotiable drivers of choice. However, as we learned in chapter 2, location is a fixed entity, and while pricing is more flexible, that is only up to a certain point. As for your product, the limits to what you can do vary from small tweaks, such as paint color or updated fixtures, to major changes, such as remodeling or construction, including the addition of new units. Where your property falls within this range depends on the fundamentals of your business, and these are typically beyond the scope of a monthly checkup. (They should be assessed on an annual basis during budget reviews.)

Still, it is vital to know your competition, to know the market in your locale, and to continually track and analyze the results of website hits and responses and, most of all, the results of inquiries and visits from prospective residents. What does your property offer? How does what you offer relate to what prospects tell you they want? And how does it relate to what the marketplace offers? The answers to these questions change with economic conditions and other factors.

What questions should you be asking, and what aspects should you be inspecting during your monthly visits?

PRODUCT CHECKLIST

1. Does the property's curb appeal make a great first impression?
2. Are the property and amenities clean?
3. **Is each model/unit clean and working properly?**
4. Is your team emphasizing the property's strong points while leasing?

1: Does the Property's Curb Appeal Make a Great First Impression?

As you know, you only have one chance to make a first impression. We must never underestimate the value placed on first impressions. Lead your team to understand that, whatever else you are selling, you are first selling an impression—and you only have one chance to make a great one that lasts.

Focus your team's attention on creating the best curb appeal possible. In addition to curb appeal, the model and show units must always be clean and impeccably maintained. Potential residents cannot ignore the drip-drip-drip of a leaky faucet, and they cannot unsee a dead bug in the sink. Nothing will stop a prospective resident from leasing more swiftly than the sight of a dirty, poorly maintained property, either inside or out. The impression this creates cuts deeper than the inherent disgust of dirt and dilapidation. These things broadcast to the prospect that no one on this property—whether staff or residents—cares about where they live or work. The staff clearly does not care how the residents live, and the residents, most likely, don't care much about one another and even less about the property. This is not a desirable *community*. In fact, it is not a community at all.

A dirty or even somewhat unkempt property and a visible indifference to maintenance creates not merely an impression of negligence, but also of discontent and danger. The *broken windows theory* is a sociological and criminological concept holding that visible signs of neglect and vandalism, such as broken windows left unrepaired, tend to encourage further disorder and even more serious crime in a neighborhood. This theory has been criticized for producing overly zealous policing, yet it does accurately portray the impression created by the visible signs of neglect and carelessness in a community. It is a gut-level impression that no one is safe here because people who do not look after their own place are not likely to care about one another. On a property, dirt, decay, and disorder are incompatible with a sense of community.

> Our first impressions are generated by our experiences and our environment, which means that we can change our first impressions . . . by changing the experiences that comprise those impressions.
>
> —MALCOLM GLADWELL

Beer-Bottle Blindness

We become blind to things we see over and over again. They recede into the background. Have you noticed that when a new billboard goes up, you see it, but after driving by it a hundred times you don't even look at it anymore?

Ken recalls when he had a new property manager on one of his properties. While she was trying hard to stay on top of all the issues at the site, Ken noticed that at the front entrance to the community, just to the side of the sign, a beer bottle had been thrown into the bushes but in plain sight. He took out his smartphone, snapped a photo of it, and checked in on the new property manager, making it a point to ask if she had noticed any issues.

"There were a few minor things. But we've addressed all of them."

"Okay," Ken said, "I just want to make sure you and the staff understand the importance of cleanliness and curb appeal. We need to make a strong first impression."

How long would it take for her—or a staff member—to see the beer bottle at the entrance? Ken came back the following week and found the bottle still there. So he asked members of the team about the grounds.

"Everything looks great!" was the general response.

That was when he whipped out his phone and showed them the picture.

"That beer bottle has been out by the front entrance sign for at least a week."

They gasped at the photo, genuinely shocked. Not one of them had seen the beer bottle! And Ken knew they weren't just saying it, because the dismay was evident on each person's face. They had all succumbed to beer-bottle blindness.

How do you avoid this plague of property management? It requires an act of will and an attitude of mindfulness. Be deliberate in your search for things that are out of place. Shake yourself out of seeing the expected by varying your routine. When you walk the property on Tuesday, walk it differently from the way you did on Monday. If you did a clockwise circuit Wednesday, take the trip counterclockwise on Thursday. This will allow you to notice details previously missed. Attention to detail is a valuable skill in property management. As the great architect Mies van der Rohe put it, "God is in the details." Teach yourself and your team to look and look closely.

Where Do You Go to the Bathroom When You're on the Road?

The drive has been long, and you and your family really need a bathroom break. You catch sight of an old gas station just to the right and also a sign telling you that a McDonald's is two miles farther down the road.

You wait the two miles. You know that a McDonald's restroom is always clean. The old gas station? Well, that's a roll of the dice.

Now, the cleanliness of a McDonald's restroom is not an accident. It is a feature of the brand, and the management makes no secret of that. Have you ever looked at the back of the door of a McDonald's restroom? Posted prominently at eye level is a checklist that shows when the bathroom was last cleaned. The manager makes a point of checking this throughout the day. The message of a clean bathroom is twofold: We care about cleanliness, and if our bathroom is this clean, you should see our kitchen! Why do we care about cleanliness? Because we care about *you*, our guest.

You can take the McDonald's example as a literal reminder to make sure the bathrooms and common public areas on your property are always clean and appropriately stocked with toilet paper, hand soap, and paper towels. But think bigger too. By ensuring that the entire property is clean, well-groomed, and impeccably maintained, you are sending a message: We care about our residents.

Curb Appeal

In real estate, the common term for everything that goes into the first impression a property makes is, of course, "curb appeal." Homeowners who put their property up for sale and want it to stand out from the rest look for ways to make a strong first impression. Realtors often advise them to increase curb appeal by pressure washing or repainting, doing some landscaping, hiding wear-and-tear on the roof by replacing torn or missing shingles, and so on. The principle is the same in making sure to create great curb appeal at the property. It's just that creating curb appeal at an apartment community must be done on a much larger scale.

The quickest way to define positive curb appeal in a rental property is to first present the negative picture—what constitutes *poor* curb appeal. We figure that the antonym of *curb appeal* must be *curb non-appeal* or maybe even *curb repulsion*. But let's just look at the following list:

The Scars of Poor Curb Appeal

- Overgrown grass and shrubs
- Weeds in the parking lot
- Trash and litter on the site
- Dumpsters, compactors, or trash cans overflowing with trash

- Window screens missing or damaged
- Torn blinds
- Broken windows
- Lights not working or broken
- Peeling or fading paint
- Damaged siding
- Drainage problems
- Areas that have no grass
- Damaged or disconnected gutters
- Undriveable cars in the parking lot
- Dirty clubhouse and/or amenities
- Damaged amenities
- Potholes in the parking lot
- Dirty signage or signage in need of repair
- Green and/or dirty pool
- Damaged fencing

It takes little effort to convert this inventory of poor curb appeal features into a checklist of action items intended to ensure great curb appeal.

Lifting Curb Appeal

- Trim and manicure overgrown grass and shrubs.
- Thoroughly weed the parking lot.
- Aggressively police any trash and litter on the site.
- Ensure that dumpsters, compactors, and trash cans are neat and tidy and never overflow with trash.
- Replace missing or damaged window screens.
- Inspect for torn blinds and replace them.

- Replace all broken windows.
- Ensure that all outdoor lighting works and replace any broken lights.
- Inspect for peeling or fading paint and repaint as needed.
- Inspect for damaged siding and repair or replace as needed.
- Access and address any drainage problems.
- Plant grass or sod in ground areas that have no grass.
- Inspect for damaged or disconnected gutters and repair or replace them as needed.
- Clear the parking lot of abandoned or undrivable cars.
- Ensure that the clubhouse and/or other amenities are clean and inviting.
- Inspect for damaged amenities and make necessary repairs and replacements.
- Walk the parking lot, note any potholes, and have them repaired.
- Inspect the property's signage and clean or repair signs as needed.
- Inspect the pool for dirty or green water and thoroughly clean and restore it to a usable, inviting, and healthy condition.
- Inspect for damaged fencing and repair or replace as needed.

Take special care to ensure that high-visibility features serve as selling points. Give prospective residents a reason to stay and look around rather than turn on their heels and run. For instance:

- Ensure that the clubhouse, if the property has one, looks its best.
- All amenities must be in good repair and well-maintained.
- All landscaping must be well-maintained.

- Make certain the marketing/model path is clean and well-maintained.
- Rigorously inspect the show units. They must be clean, well-maintained, and rent ready.
- Signage and promotional materials must represent the property the way you want it to be represented.
- The rental office is typically the first interior space a prospective resident sees and the final stop before he or she fills out an application or signs an agreement. Ensure that the office is clean and inviting. Restrooms in the rental facility must be clean and properly stocked.

2: Are the Property and Amenities Clean?

If the property's curb appeal makes a favorable impression and prospective residents tour the property/amenities and some units, what do they see? It's easy enough to find out. Take a tour. See what the prospect sees.

Property Inspection

The inspection of a unit begins on your way to the unit. Look at the sidewalks, the parking lot, and the stairs. See anything *you* don't like? Trash, weeds, overgrown grass, peeling paint, damaged windows? Cracked sidewalks? Damaged or worn stairs? Handrails missing or handrails that are not attached properly? Rust? Flaking paint?

What makes you *uncomfortable*? Does anything cause you to blink or make you feel embarrassed? These are the very things that will turn off a potential resident.

When you inspect a property, you are looking first and foremost for things that need to be fixed. When a potential resident is looking, whether they need a place fast or are in no hurry, that individual may be searching for a reason to fall in love with the place or may be searching for a reason to say no. The truth is that most prospects are driven by both motives. Your job is to do all you can to create desire and overcome objections. Start by correcting any issues in need of correction. Clean up, spruce up, repaint, and make repairs. These steps eliminate the major sources of objection. Do this, and you will gain the confidence you need to make a great first impression, tipping the balance toward "I love it and I'll take it."

Exterior doors

While you are standing at the entrance to the unit, take a few moments to look at the exterior of the front door.

Look at the condition of the paint. Look at the condition of any glass in the door. Both should be flawless and clean. Doors get dirty—handprints and, yes, even shoeprints. They also collect dirt at the bottom. None of that should be present when a prospect arrives.

Now, check for gaps around the weather stripping's edges. If lights are on inside, can you see any light coming through? You will want to check for this while you are still outside but also once you are inside the unit and have closed the door behind you. Can you see daylight anywhere along the perimeter of the door? If so, that means air is leaking in and out of the unit. This will make a heating and cooling system work harder, which results in one thing: a higher utility bill for your residents. Ours is an era of tight-fitting doors, double-pane windows, and well-sealed joints. Residents expect that level of construction and maintenance.

What you see as you open and close the exterior door is only part of the impression this architectural feature makes on a prospect. Notice: Does the door open and close properly? Does the door stick when it is opened or closed? Or does it open smoothly and close effortlessly? Do you have to slam it shut? Or does it click neatly into place?

When you turn the key in the lock, is the response smooth and flawless the very first time? Check the doorknob and the deadbolt. Do they work correctly? What the question really means is: Do they work flawlessly? Is there any play in either the doorknob or the twist lever for the deadbolt? There should not be.

People who make a living selling cars know how a door that feels effortless on opening and solid on closing will help sell a vehicle. It speaks of craftsmanship, which speaks of caring, which speaks of value. Think about this when you open and close the door of the unit you are inspecting.

Hallways and breezeways

This is your resident's first impression. Check to make sure the flooring is not damaged and that everything is clean, with no debris or personal belongings in the common areas. The door into a common hallway should have a doorstop of some sort to keep it from damaging the wall. Make sure it is there and functional. A prospect who opens the door only to have it hit the wall may complete the tour, but he or she likely won't do so with the memory of a favorable first impression. Check that the hallway/breezeway lights are working correctly.

Windows

We all love to have lots of windows in our living space. If the view is pretty—great! But even if it is ordinary, it needs to be clean and pleasant. This includes the condition of the windows. Prospective residents imagine themselves using the windows, looking out, and enjoying the light.

Windows must be clean. They must be properly maintained. Do not show a unit with broken panes. Showing such a unit is self-sabotage. Apologizing for the broken pane—"Sorry, we will fix it!"—only deepens the negative impression. The prospect will feel offended at having been shown a home with a broken window. Only a little less offensive are panes with obvious gaps along any edge or panes that are not firmly set in their frames. When you're inspecting, push on the glass. There should be no movement.

Push down on the windows as well. This will give you a good indication of whether they are loose and therefore in need of repair. Take another close look at window seals. Inspect for excessive moisture or, even more critically, for mildew. These are signs of condensation or even exterior water leaks. Not only should such windows be tagged for repair or replacement, but also any mold or mildew needs to be completely cleaned. Potential residents know that mold is not healthy.

Depending on where you live, screens in front of the windows can be critically important. Inspect the screens on every window. They must have no holes, tears, bulges, indentations, spiderwebs, or bugs.

Porches and decks

Porches and decks can really make an apartment feel like home, and they are great selling points—unless they are anything less than perfect. In terms of appearance, the paint should be clean and in great shape. Floors should be clean and undamaged. Signs of water damage are especially strong turnoffs for prospects.

Next, check any railings for stability. The same goes for gates and fences.

Porches and decks extend outward. Now is the time to take a good look at any trees surrounding the apartment. We all love trees, but you need to trim back branches that may be touching the buildings or roofs.

3: Is Each Model or Unit Clean and Working Properly?

Time to get more closely acquainted with the unit you are inspecting.

Sniff Out Potential Objections

Close your eyes for a moment and sniff the air. Our sense of smell is a powerful driver of emotion, sensation, and action. We are attracted by lowkey pleasant aromas and repelled by unpleasant odors. Our response goes deeper than that, of course. Some bad smells speak volumes, especially when we are investigating a new or unfamiliar environment.

What do you want to smell?

A vacant unit should smell clean. This does not mean that it should smell like bleach or disinfectant. Nobody wants to smell these things, and if these odors are in the air, prospective residents are likely to assume that you are trying to cover up some other smell.

Room deodorizer scents are not to everyone's taste— room deodorizers suggest that you have something to hide. So, in fact, the best answer to the question, "What do you want to smell in a vacant apartment?" is, "Nothing, nothing at all." The best way a vacant apartment can smell is neutral.

Sniff it out

When you inspect a unit and something doesn't smell right, investigate.

Plumbing gas. If a clean vacant unit smells like a sewer or reminds you of rotten eggs, the most likely source is water in the shower and sink drains evaporating over time. The U-shaped trap in the piping that goes down from a drain and, ultimately, leads out to the sewer system is designed to hold water, which acts as a seal against seepage of sewer gas into the residence. If the plumbing is not used for a time, the water in the trap can evaporate, thus breaking the seal and allowing sewer gas to seep in. The first thing to try is simply to run the water in all the sinks in the unit, air the place out, and come back later. If the smell is gone, you have addressed the problem successfully. If not, you need to call your maintenance supervisor, who will call in a plumber to track the source of the problem. Typically, a blockage or leak in the plumbing vent stack is the culprit.

Sewer gas not only makes a unit unrentable, but it may also make it virtually unlivable. A buildup of hydrogen sulfide gas, a main ingredient of sewer gas, is not only rotten-egg noxious but also toxic. Sewer gas odors may be signs of a plumbing backup as well. These signs must not be ignored but thoroughly investigated.

Mildew, mold, and other musty smells. If the unit smells moldy—that dank, sharp odor that makes any enclosed space instantly feel like a Stephen King novel—the first step is to track down the mold or mildew causing the odor. Eliminate the source, and you will eliminate the odor. If mold and mildew are persistent in a unit, check the washer and dryer connections, the dishwasher drain, the HVAC drain pan, and around all the windows for any active leaks. Depending on the variety, mold is unhealthy and in rare cases is potentially life-threatening, so it helps to act with the appropriate urgency.

If the unit has a strong smell of mildew and you cannot find any visible signs of mold and mildew or detect the presence of an active water leak, you need to use a moisture meter to check the walls for hidden leaks. It's a good idea to start your search wherever the odor is strongest. Bear in mind that mold and mildew don't just materialize anywhere. They need three things to develop and grow: a source of moisture, a medium on which to grow, and the right temperature. The most common indoor mildews and molds grow most successfully at temperatures between 55 and 85 degrees Fahrenheit. Some species, however, will grow at any temperature. Find the source and correct the problem.

Pet odors. Personally, we love pets, but let's face it, like all of us, they are producers of pervasive odors. In the case of pets, these can range from litter box smells, to dog or cat urine that has soaked into the carpet padding and even the grain of hardwood floors. Sometimes we even detect that vague yet unmistakable "wet dog" smell. From the standpoint of a property manager, the real problem with pet odors is that they don't go away with the pet. They linger—often stubbornly.

When you inspect a unit and detect the lingering odors of pets, the first thing to do is ensure that the previous furry resident has left no unwanted presents behind. Once this is addressed, look at the unit's carpeting and, if the unit is furnished, the upholstered furniture. A standard commercial-grade carpet cleaning may mitigate or even cure the problem. Your carpet cleaning company should use a neutralizer product that is specially designed to minimize pet odors. If, however, the smell is predominantly of urine, it is likely that the source has penetrated so deeply that at least some portions of the carpeting will have to be discarded and replaced. In worst-case scenarios, you may even have to resort to professional HVAC duct cleanings or install an ozone machine for a period of time in order to get back to the neutral odor new residents desire.

Once you're done checking and you've gotten rid of all smells left behind by pets, it may be a good time to review your policy and pricing for pet owners.

Smoke odor. Some residential communities have smoke-free policies or offer leases with and without no-smoking addendums. For a variety of reasons, the ideal situation is a smoke-free property, but this is not always possible or feasible. From the perspective of the value of a unit, smoke odors are strong negatives for most prospects, and those odors are very difficult to remove. Smoke soaks into most surfaces and carpeting and even gets into the HVAC system. You will need to take special cleaning steps to remove the smells from the carpet, paint, and HVAC system. Just as with pet odors, you may even consider having the HVAC ducts cleaned since odors can become trapped in the ducts and continue to circulate throughout the unit. Sometimes the odor may call for you to install an ozone unit for a period of time to actively remove odor particles from the air. Finally, repainting the interior of the unit can be a highly effective measure.

Bathrooms

Bathrooms are intimate spaces and a location in which prospective residents are usually acutely sensitive to the slightest indication of uncleanliness. On the other hand, an astonishingly clean bathroom will leave a great impression as a prospective resident evaluates a unit. So as you tour the unit, make no compromises about the appearance and condition of the bathroom. Touring prospective residents will probably not be using the bathrooms in the models, but they should view them as fully functional and *ready* to use.

Toilets. Check that the toilet seat is sturdy. The seats are easy to tighten, but they do need to be tightened from time to time. Look at the condition of the seat. New seats are not expensive, and they can be easily installed.

Flush the toilet—more than once. Watch to make sure the bowl refills as it should and that the toilet stops running after a brief amount of time. The second flush will tell you how long the toilet needs to reset. Look around the base of the toilet and behind it. Make sure all connections are secure and there are no active signs of leaks.

Showers and bathtubs. If you have a tub-shower combo, turn it on, and check that the appropriate switch works. Make sure water can come out of both the showerhead and the bath faucet. Put your hand in the water stream to judge if it has enough pressure, that the water is sufficiently hot, and that the temperature adjusts appropriately.

Make sure the drain works properly and efficiently. The drain should appear immaculate. If the chrome or other coating is chipping or if corrosion is evident, replace the screen over the drain, especially in the shower/bathtub. When you turn the water off, watch and listen for any residual water drips, and wait to see how long it keeps dripping. If it keeps dripping, make certain to get the drip repaired.

Again, check for signs of mold and mildew. Give the grout an especially close look.

Sinks and cabinets. Turn on all sink faucets in the unit and check for water pressure and temperature. Note how long it takes for the temperature to adjust. Open the cabinet vanities and examine the plumbing underneath. Note any leaks, cracks, mold, or other damage.

Most bathrooms come with cabinets and drawers. Check cabinet doors and drawers to make sure they open and close properly. Look for paint chipping and cracks. Repair as needed.

Do All Appliances Work, and Do Cabinets and Drawers Function as Designed?

Refrigerator. Even if the fridge looks good on the outside, open it up. Does the stripping properly seal and unseal? How about the lighting? Do the lights turn on and off as you open and close the door? Put your hand inside the refrigerator, and then switch over to the freezer. Make sure that you feel an appropriate temperature shift between these two sections.

Inspect the trays and shelves in the fridge. Are they in good condition? Is anything broken, bent, or flimsy? Are any parts of the interior cracked? If the appliance has an ice maker, take a look at the ice it produces. Make certain that the ice maker is producing ice properly. Most importantly, if the ice maker is not working, make a note and have it repaired.

Dishwasher. Open the dishwasher and turn it on while you continue to inspect the unit. Make sure it is working and that all pieces, such as racks and utensil baskets, are present. There should be no damage, dirt, or gunk buildup inside.

Oven and stove. If you have a stove with gas burners, check all of them and make sure that they work. There should be absolutely no smell of gas. Look at the burner grates and ensure that there is no buildup of grease. Check the drip pans around the burners and make sure that they are clean and undamaged.

Look inside the oven and evaluate its cleanliness and overall condition. Turn it on, and make sure that it starts without a problem.

If the kitchen has an electric stove, turn on each burner to ensure that they all work.

Kitchen cabinets and drawers. Kitchen cabinets and drawers, where food and utensils are kept, are also likely places for bugs to hide. Open all drawers and cabinets. Use a flashlight to check for evidence of pests. Also, laser in on any cracks or holes, which provide entryways for pests. While you are at it, look around for water damage or cracks. Do not neglect to note any damage to the cabinet doors, from chipped paint to a broken hinge. Remedy any problems before showing the apartment. Evidence of pests will stop a prospect cold, as will shoddy cabinet doors and drawers.

A lack of care for the quality and presentation of any of the above-listed items will broadcast negligence. Again, inspect what you expect and make a great first impression!

Inspect the Utility Closet

HVAC Systems and Water Heaters

No one expects you to be an HVAC or plumbing expert, but in your monthly inspection of vacant units, always include the HVAC system. The only thing needed is the ability to set the thermostat low enough to turn the AC on and then put your hand over a few of the registers to check for cool air. Once this is done, turn the thermostat up high enough to turn on the heat. Check the registers. Often, there is a built-in time delay between when you set the thermostat and when the system kicks in, so be sure to allow for that. The delay may be a moment or several minutes, depending on the system and its settings.

You should know where the system's air filter is located and how to access the filter. Check its condition. Your maintenance team should be changing filters on a fixed schedule. While you are accessing the HVAC unit, inspect the primary vent, ensuring that it looks well maintained. Most HVAC air handlers and coil units are set in a condensation pan, which is designed to catch any air conditioning condensation that does not go out the drain line as it should. The pan should have no standing water in it. If it does, you can take a quick look for leaks or a stopped-up drain, but you will need to notify your maintenance supervisor so that the issue can be corrected. Condensation pans are notorious for growing algae and mold. The condensation pan should be fitted with a float switch, which turns off the A/C if the pan is about to overflow due to a clogged drain. An overflow can result in water damage, not only to this unit but also to the unit below it. If you feel comfortable with your level of expertise, inspect the float switch. If not, make certain that inspection is being regularly done by the maintenance team.

Look at the condition of registers or vents throughout the apartment. They should be rust-free, chip-free, and dust-free.

Access the unit's water heater and look for leaks. Rust or corrosion anywhere on the water tank or pipes is a sign of imminent failure. Be sure to immediately notify your maintenance supervisor of your findings.

Electrical System

Inspecting the electrical system should consist mainly of heading over to the light switches and turning them on and off a few times. For any switches that have a dimmer, ensure that it is fully functional. While the lights are on, turn on either the air conditioning or a heavy appliance. Flickering of lights may indicate an electrical problem in the unit that needs to be addressed by the maintenance supervisor or a member of their team.

Take the time to look for any burned-out bulbs. Note them and ensure that they are replaced before the unit is shown. You should also access the circuit breaker box. Open it and look for any tripped breakers. Unless you know that the breaker is in the off position for an intentional reason, notify your maintenance supervisor.

County or city codes and ordinances may apply to the smoke and carbon monoxide detectors and fire extinguishers. Make certain they are in working condition and are up to code with the proper inspections required. Know what is required by applicable regulations. Heavily consider employing a certified inspection company to do, at minimum, annual inspections of detectors and extinguishers.

Furniture

If you offer furnished units, the condition of the furniture in the apartment becomes either a major attraction or a major turn-off.

Check the furniture, making sure that any of your cloth pieces (mattresses, bar stools, couches, and so on) are not stained or ripped. Is any furniture chipped or scratched? Are any parts of the furniture missing?

Make certain that all furniture is accounted for and that the furniture is structurally stable. Also assess whether the furniture looks reasonably new and therefore really is an added value for the price you are offering. If you think the furniture in a unit adds no value or, worse, detracts from value, assess the situation. You may want to lower the rental price, rent the unit unfurnished, or buy new furniture.

Tools for Property Inspection

1. Ensure that your team is taking thorough notes when walking a property—whether on an iPad (or another tablet), iPhone or Android, or with a pen and paper. Make certain that property records are being made. As the old Chinese proverb puts it, "The faintest ink is more powerful than the strongest memory." Mental notes are not sufficient.

2. Staff should make ample use of their iPhone or Android cameras to document the condition of the property, especially any damage or other problems. Google Photos (https://photos.google.com/) is great for backing up your documentary photos from inspection walks. It's free, it will keep your visual records orderly and accessible, and it will save storage space on your mobile phone.

3. AirTable (https://airtable.com) is a great online database product which will allow you to import your spreadsheets into a database and attach photos and PDFs from your inspection. It is easy to use and very effective.

    There are many other excellent tools, such as PropertyInspect.com, Snapinspect.com, and Happy.com. More are being built and developed all the time. If you have a large group of properties, some of these inspection apps will enable much better tracking of action items.

4: Is Your Leasing Team Emphasizing the Advantages of the Property?

The key to selling successfully is knowing your product intimately as well as what typically motivates someone to become a customer. It's important to know what sets you apart from competitors and be able to overcome the objections of prospective residents with persuasive alternatives. For example, if a prospect prefers a property with a gym and spa but those aren't amenities you offer, instead point out the jogging trail on the property's perimeter, the availability of gyms at nearby shopping centers, and the bike trail at the county park. Focus on your main selling points when marketing and cultivating prospects, such as location or floorplan size.

Playing to your strengths is not just about emphasizing the pluses of the property; it is about making the most of the *whole* property.

Remember, when people are looking for a place to live, they run through an internal checklist or wish list. This is the way they screen what your property has to offer. Price and location are foundational. If your property is significantly beyond the budget of the prospective resident, nothing you do can change that. The same goes for location. If your property is distant from the prospect's workplace or must-have school, or if it is remote from desirable shopping, you will not convert that prospect to a resident. If, however, the price is within range and the location is acceptable, the prospect's decision will be based on things like the specifics of available units, cleanliness and maintenance, amenities, and a great staff. Never underestimate the importance of a great staff in a prospect's final leasing decision.

All these features and factors can be spelled out and presented in ads or by sales associates. They are tangible, even quantifiable.

Summary

Our third *P, product*, is the most tangible aspect of the rental property. Owners, management company personnel, and on-site staff need to look at every aspect of the property through the eyes (and nose!) of both current and prospective residents. The objective is to ensure that the product makes a great first impression and is always reflected in the best possible way.

Exterior walks to check the buildings from the rooftops to the foundations should happen at a minimum on a quarterly basis. The manager and maintenance supervisor should both be involved in these two inspection processes. If your property does not have a staff member assigned to monitor inspection processes, it is urgent that you make the assignment. At the end of the day, the attention and respect you pay to your product represent to your residents and prospects the attention and respect they can expect to receive as well.

CHAPTER 4

The Fourth P Is for Promotion

> *Half the money I spend on advertising is wasted; the trouble is I don't know which half.*
>
> —JOHN WANAMAKER

Marketing and advertising are two of the most integral systems we put in place for our properties. These are critical parts of telling prospects "who we are" and thus essential to creating a sense of urgency in those who are looking for a new home. Marketing and advertising must reflect the imperative to lease quickly to avoid missing out on a great special or floorplan. To be effective, these essential activities must be carried out consistently and correctly and updated often.

If marketing and advertising are not being handled effectively, occupancy will drop and the bottom line will suffer. Prospective residents will not be moved to action, leasing activity will slow down, and rental and other income will decrease. So it's important to stay constantly focused on creating the results you want. An online presence is critical, and you must monitor your online advertising closely and systematically to ensure that you are not missing anything important.

PROMOTION CHECKLIST

1. Review your current marketing plan.
2. Review lead-tracking software.

- Check closing ratios.
- Check follow-ups.
- Check inactive calls.
- Listen to sample leasing calls.
- Compare leads.

3. What is the competition doing?
4. Review paid ad programs.
5. Check Google reviews and other promotional sites.
6. Evaluate your property's website.

1: Review Your Current Marketing Plan

In any enterprise, a marketing plan is an operational document outlining an advertising strategy to reach your targeted market, generate leads, and attract potential customers. The marketing plan details the advertising and other outreach campaigns that are to be implemented over a specified period. The plan should provide a means of measuring the effectiveness of the various components of the campaigns.

Any marketing plan should include specifications for the following:

- Market research, which is needed to inform and support pricing decisions
- A rationale for your choice of advertising platforms. The so-called *marketing mix* will include digital platforms (such as Apartments.com, Apartmentguide.com, Google, and Bing)

and social media platforms (such as Facebook, Snapchat, Instagram, and TikTok) as well as email blasts and even direct mail.

- Messaging tailored to key relevant demographics and geographical areas.
- Methods of reporting and analyzing the effectiveness of all these marketing channels.

2: Review Lead-Tracking Software

There are many popular brands of lead-tracking software, such as Lease Hawk and I Love Leasing. However, many of the property-management software programs have lead-tracking software already built into them. Reviewing the lead-tracking capabilities in your program plays an integral role in the *promotion* checklist.

If your property does not have lead-tracking software or the capability to monitor the leasing leads, then it is impossible to manage the promotion and leasing processes. A property without the ability to track leads is at an automatic disadvantage when it comes to the ability to monitor the success or lack thereof.

- **Check closing ratios.** A *closing ratio* is simply the percentage of actual leases divided by the total number of leads. This can be further broken down into individual leasing agent closing ratios using the same formula. For example: a property with one hundred leads and twenty-five leases would have a closing ratio of 25 percent (25/100 = 0.25; 0.25 x 100 = 25%). If the same property had two leasing agents, you would allocate the number each individual had in leads vs. actual leases to determine their personal closing ratios.

o A good rule of thumb is an individual closing ratio of 15–25 percent. However, always look for extremes one way or another and investigate. Data could be incorrect or manipulated in either case, whether the percentages are extremely high or low. Lead tracking software will generate reports that automatically provide this information.

- **Check on follow-ups.** Follow-up is one of the most critical parts of the leasing agent position. A leasing agent should be consistently and constantly sending text messages and emails and making phone calls to potential residents. Lead-tracking software will provide accurate information on follow-ups: which leasing agents are following up on 100 percent of their leads and which ones are not. The goal of each leasing agent is 100 percent follow-up. Follow-up is the easiest way to increase the closing ratio.

  o **Check stalled leads.** A stalled lead is a lead that has not had follow-up activity or any contact with the leasing staff in the past forty-eight hours. It is important to monitor the stalled leads on the property, as each lead is a potential new move-in.

- **Check inactive and non-prospect calls.** This area is one of the easiest to manipulate. In addition, if you are getting several non-prospect calls, your advertising will need to be adjusted accordingly. For example: if you are getting a number of prospects looking for a one-bedroom unit and you only offer two- and three-bedroom units, there is a problem that needs to be addressed immediately. On the other hand, if a closing ratio is affected by this report, further investigations need to take place.

o **Listen to sample leasing calls.** All leasing calls coming through the marketing phone numbers are recorded by the software. A good training tool is to listen to a sample of these calls for each leasing agent and to make certain that calls are being handled in accordance with company policy.

- **Compare leads.** Look for trends or problems with various sources by checking leads month over month and year over year. If, for example, last year in January you had two hundred leads and this January you only have one hundred leads, you need to adjust your marketing strategy. This is a great early indicator that you may have issues that need to be addressed.

3: What Is the Competition Doing?

The ability to learn faster than your competitors may be the only sustainable competitive advantage.

—ARIE DE GEUS

The importance of knowing what your competitors are doing is hardly unique to the leasing industry, but this knowledge **is so critical to the success of marketing that this topic, raised in the pricing chapter, chapter 2, is revisited here.**

Depending on where your property or properties are located, prospects may have a wide range of offerings to choose from.

Remember, your prospective residents are most constrained by two variables: location and price. At a minimum, the property they choose must be located in convenient or at least feasible proximity to such things as workplaces, schools, shopping centers, and transportation (bus stops, rapid transit lines, highways, airports, and so on). The property must also fit into the renter's budget.

These same two variables, location and price, constrain the property owner or manager as well. The location of the property is a given, which means that you may have to take steps to inform and educate consumers about the benefits of the location. As for pricing, you typically have some room to maneuver, but there is always a break-even point. Increasing or decreasing the rent can be a slippery slope, especially in a highly competitive market. No one can afford to overprice or underprice their units. This means you must know what your competitors are offering. What prices and what incentives are they offering? Armed with this knowledge, you can plan your marketing campaigns accordingly. You need to know how to present—compellingly—both the hard variables (location and price) and the more competitive features (aesthetics, amenities, and so on).

Market surveys and secret shopping are the two tools most widely used in the leasing industry to evaluate both your property and its performance, as well as what the competition is doing. You must, of course, assume that your competitors are using the same evaluative tools to also scope out *your* property. This mutual surveillance often makes for a very fluid market. Answering the question, "What are your competitors doing?" requires continual monitoring. The likelihood is that whatever you saw a competitor doing last week, that may be different this week. The market is constantly changing.

Every property manager should conduct market surveys on a *weekly* basis. These surveys are based on leasing statistics, specials offered, and any changes to rates or amenities. (See the pricing chapter, chapter 2, for further details.) If your property does not have a weekly market survey routine in place, it is high time that you start. Stop operating in the dark.

Competition Shopping

Good property managers learn the market in which their properties exist. They don't go to school for this knowledge. They teach themselves by identifying the comps—properties at comparable price points with features and benefits comparable to their own property— and then shopping them personally.

Pay special attention to how your property stacks up against the competition, especially in terms of finishes, amenities offered, and the appearance of the grounds. The objective is less to gauge the appeal of the competitor's property than it is to make sure *your* site is not obviously lacking in some way, especially in the most conspicuous features. For instance, if all your comps offer washers and dryers and you do not, you will be perceived—quite correctly—as offering less value than the competition. Unless your location is superior to the comps, your only competitive choices are likely lowering your prices or buying the appliances.

Property managers should be regularly shopping the comps as a matter of habit. But also analyze the market surveys and ask yourself whether any competitor stands out from the rest. Are they consistently reporting higher leasing numbers than the market average dictates? Investigate to find out why.

This is a signal that it may be time to more thoroughly secret shop that competitor. *Secret*—or *mystery*—*shopping* is a technique that market research companies and others use to test any number of things, such as the quality of sales or service, job performance, and so on. In our industry, secret shopping is used to gather firsthand information about specific competitors.

Secret shopping is mainly used as a training tool for your own staff. However, it can be used as an investigative tool when needed.

If you are managing a property, a simple phone call may be all you need. Posing as a prospective residents, call a competing property and ask the questions any prospect would ask. Or you can send someone to make an in-person visit. You might send a new employee, one who is not known by the competitor. Whether on the phone or with a visit, the secret shopper contacts the competing property from the perspective of an interested prospect. There is nothing illegal or unethical about this. After all, you are just looking and asking for information that is offered to any potential resident. Also, despite the adjective modifying the word *shopper*, there is nothing truly secret about this market research tactic, which is widely used throughout the residential leasing industry.

Your secret shopper should specifically ask for information on specials and rates. You should then compare the secret shopper information to whatever the property has shared with you in your weekly market survey. In a perfect world, everyone would accurately share their information, but in the highly competitive world of residential leasing, properties occasionally run flash specials they do not share with you when asked during a market survey.

Shopping the competition is beneficial in the training of any new leasing employee. It affords an opportunity to gain firsthand knowledge about the market and your competitors. Most importantly, it allows you to gain insight from the perspective of prospects. It is always a valuable advantage to see your product from the perspective of your customer. The experience will help new employees to provide more accurate, specific, and persuasive information to prospects who visit or call about your property. All new employees should secretly shop their main competitors as part of the training process. Knowing the differences when working with prospects who are trying to make a decision is key.

Shopping the competition also exposes new employees to the sales techniques of others. It is a way to increase their own sales skills, especially if they have had some solid sales training by the time the competition shopping begins. Good salespeople are always on the hunt for new approaches. Learning to sell by being sold to is an extremely effective means of learning new and/or additional sales techniques.

4: Review Paid Ad Programs

Let's begin by making sure we are speaking the same language. "Marketing" and "sales" are often used interchangeably. They should not be—at least not in business. While both marketing and sales impact lead generation and revenue, they denote two distinct business functions within an organization.

Marketing is the process of getting consumers interested in whatever you are selling. *Sales* refers to all your business activities that lead to the actual sale of goods and services. Marketing includes all activities intended to spark interest in your business and to create a buzz. Toward this end, marketing uses some form of market research and analysis to understand the interests, wants, and needs of potential customers. Marketers create and conduct campaigns to attract consumers to a brand, product, or service.

Sales is best understood by understanding what salespeople do. They manage relationships with prospects and present to them a product or solution that culminates in a sale. Another way to think about the difference between marketing and sales is to note that marketing focuses its efforts on the more general public or large groups of people, whereas sales targets smaller groups, specific subsets of the general public, or, very often, individual prospects. You might think of *marketing* as a funnel that gathers and directs individual prospects to *sales*.

Types of Marketing

Marketing comes in many forms, especially in our ever-changing and expanding digital world. We've found it to be a best practice to engage in multiple forms of marketing at once so that you're covering all of your bases. Below we have a brief description of various types of marketing that we have found effective.

Outreach

Outreach marketing is exactly what it sounds like, physically leaving the office and marketing in a public setting. This can range from tabling at a local event, hanging up flyers at local community areas, and passing out frisbees at dog parks, to sponsoring a trivia night and even chalking sidewalks around local businesses or schools with your property name and contact information. This is a great way to get in some immediate face time rather than having to wait until someone comes in for a tour. This technique can create the ability to cultivate a connection while answering most of their questions. There are some downsides to outreach marketing though. It typically requires the most preparation and legwork, but if you have the time and staffing to attempt outreach marketing, don't be afraid to be creative. It can be beneficial in certain situations, such as events where a group of potential prospects will be gathering.

E-blast

Once you have cultivated a strong prospect pool, it's important to keep everyone up to date with any new specials, rates, or availability changes. Invest in a system that allows you to send out bulk emails, typically a flashy graphic meant to create a sense of urgency. While less personal than reaching out to each individual prospect, it is cost-effective. The popularity of the e-blast continues to decline as more tech-savvy generations move into the general prospect pool, as they are less likely to regularly check and actually read all of their emails. Spam filters also play a big role in the current effectiveness of this type of marketing.

Mailers

While not as common a marketing tactic as they used to be, direct mailers are still a go-to strategy in some markets. The biggest hurdle is creating a large enough list of viable addresses for a direct mailer to be effective. This said, we all know how quickly we personally skim through and toss junk mail, so we wouldn't necessarily recommend this technique as the most cost-effective option.

Apartment listing sites

There are several apartment listing websites available. Currently, the most popular ones are Apartments.com, RentPath.com, or Zumper.com. However, the best way to find out which one is the most popular in your market is to simply Google search "apartments" and see what source comes up first.

Prospective residents can search by floorplans, amenities, locations, and rates, and then browse your listing to look at photos and read about what you have to offer. The biggest item to remember when advertising on one of these sites is to actively keep your listing updated as rates or specials change. Many of the property-management software platforms will automatically update these websites whenever changes are made to your pricing in your system.

Social media

Social media has become a large part of marketing and resident retention, specifically within the past ten or so years. The marketing of apartments originally started out with just Facebook. Most properties now actively use Instagram, Twitter, Snapchat, TikTok, and more. Updating social media can help maintain a positive connection with prospects and residents, as well as create an image of being an appealing and fun place to live. You also have the option of paying to promote specific posts. This can increase your following as long as you are posting what people find interesting. There are a lot of resources out there regarding how to post successfully as a business on social media. A good rule to follow is always to post pictures of people. Everyone loves seeing themselves, so if you post pictures of your residents or prospects, they're far more likely to engage with you.

Search engine optimization (SEO)

We are by no means experts at SEO but would highly recommend investing immediately in a company to manage yours. As the world steadily moves more online, the majority of your prospects are going to come from people typing into a search engine looking for apartments in your area. SEO management is what puts you at the top of that list of results, rather than hoping that prospects scroll down far enough to find your website. This is one of the leading sources of advertising and prospect cultivation, and it's only going to get more competitive.

Check out this great checklist (from Backlinko, at https://back-linko.com/seo-site-audit) for your SEO on your properties:

- Step #1: Check to see if your site is mobile-friendly.
- Step #2: Make sure Google indexes one version of your website.
- Step #3: Speed up your site.
- Step #4: Find and delete "zombie pages."
- Step #5: Find and fix indexing problems.
- Step #6: Check your organic traffic.
- Step #7: Improve your on-page SEO.
- Step #8: Set up keyword rank tracking.
- Step #9: Analyze your backlinks.
- Step #10: Fix broken links.
- Step #11: Do a competitor analysis.
- Step #12: Make your content 10x better.
- Step #13: Optimize for UX signals.
- Step #14: Flatten your website architecture.
- Step #15: Launch a skyscraper post.

The Backlinko website has lots of useful links to tools to help you check your website's SEO.

Word of mouth

Word of mouth, a great but underrated form of marketing, is much harder to control in that it's based on the customers' impression of you and experience with you. Customer service is extremely important from the very beginning of the leasing process all the way through until the day they receive their final account statement. You must always maintain a good reputation. The last thing you want is a negative Google review or someone specifically posting bad comments about your property when asked in a public forum. You can also increase positive word of mouth by asking that current residents post a review. Offering referral incentives to your current residents is another way to create a positive review. Once the person they referred moves in, provide them with a gift, and again, ask for them to write a review.

Customer Service (CS)

As mentioned above, great customer service (CS) plays a huge part in running a successful property. You could have the best location, rates, and amenities in the area, but if you're known for being a miserable management company to work with, then you will undoubtedly lose leases. We briefly touched on the attitude of your staff in the first chapter, but along with a great attitude needs to be great training and sales aptitude. To get an accurate idea of the experience your prospects and residents are receiving, use the following two methods.

Secret shopping (CS)

Almost exactly the same as secret shopping your competitor, it can be equally beneficial to secret shop your own property. There are several companies specifically tailored to secret shopping communities, and they will provide you with a full report, and often even a video, of their experience throughout the process. They call the property to assess their phone skills and then come in for a tour. They will then fill out an evaluation and give a score to the member of the team that they worked with. This is a great tool, as it will provide feedback that can be used for further training. These reports can make you aware of areas that are great as well as those that may need to be worked on.

Call audits

Ideally, you should be using a customer relationship management (CRM) system with potential residents. Contracting one that will not only provide tracking numbers for your marketing sources but also will record any incoming phone calls so they can be reviewed later is critical. Conducting an audit of your recorded phone calls to evaluate the phone techniques of your leasing staff can be quite useful in training. It's best to have a checklist prepared, and then rate the calls based on which points or information they may or may not have discussed or collected. This checklist should include the following:

- The prospect's name and contact information.
- How soon they are looking to move.
- Which floorplan they are interested in.
- An overview of the current specials and rates.
- A mention of the amenities.
- An attempt to schedule a tour.
- How they heard about the property.
- Check for a record of the agent's follow-up with the prospect after the call.

Promotion

Promotion should create a call to action that gets prospects to respond.

Promotion is a participation—not a spectator—sport. You need to be active and proactive, continuously monitoring and adjusting your messaging. This means not only watching what works but also watching for what doesn't.

Promotion can be a double-edged sword. You want to ensure that you not only get noticed but also get noticed for the right things. If prospects are not being called to action, then it is time to change your message.

Wasted dollars and dead leads

Ken had a problem. The property was not getting enough leads, and no one could figure out why. So he asked the regional manager and her team to get copies of all ads for his review. At the time, print media was still a major advertising outlet, so he called for both print and digital media ads.

Ken began by calling all the phone numbers in the ads. Each advertisement had its own number, so listening to calls was easy. He placed the calls on speakerphone, and in a few minutes, the team understood the reason for the drop in leads. The call-tracking numbers were going directly to the site voice mail. The callers were not reaching the leasing agents. If you are a potential resident trying to get information on a possible home, you want to speak with someone now. You do not want to leave a message. You hang up and call the next property.

Prospective customers don't want to leave voice mails. They want, and expect, to speak to a human being. In this case, that was not happening. In other words, Ken and his team had wasted money for a month. There were a lot of dead leads because of a change in the marketing numbers. Now you know why it is so important to assume nothing when you do your marketing audit on a site. Check the address, amenities, pricing, application fees, phone numbers, e-mails, and text messages, all social media, and so on. Make certain that all information in an advertisement is correct and working.

One picture really is worth a thousand words. (Just make sure they are the words you want.)

Few things will turn away a potential resident faster than seeing a bad photo of your property on your ads or websites. If bare earth is showing in your grassy areas, don't use the photo. If an interior unit photo shows a damaged countertop, use a different photograph. Unfavorable lighting or a bad angle can make a lovely apartment look gloomy, dingy, dirty, and small.

Photographing your property is not a job for an amateur. Invest in the services of a professional photographer. The results will more than pay for themselves in increased leasing. Look online at sites such as thumbtack.com (https://www.thumbtack.com/) and photosesh.com (https://www.photosesh.com/). Examine the sample work with a critical eye. You want to hire photographers with real estate experience and a proven track record who know how to handle lighting, angles, and details. For online ads, consider adding video tours and drone footage of your site. A moving aerial perspective injects excitement into your property and really gives your website an interesting focal piece.

5: Check Google Reviews and Other Review Sites

We all consult reviews when purchasing items online. We want to get an idea of what actual customers are saying about a product or service before we click our cash away. Even as we rely on reviews, most of us are aware that reviews can be faked and bought. Conversely, irate customers can do a hit job on your property, or a disgruntled employee can do damage by placing bad reviews. So monitor your reviews carefully and often.

Even though property managers cannot control everything that goes into the reviews they receive, it is both possible and necessary to do whatever you can to increase the odds of generating favorable reviews.

First, make sure you invite reviews. Most prospective customers want to read recent reviews when deciding on whether or not to contact a property. If your property has not elicited a review in more than three months, find out why.

Provide great customer service. Nothing creates a dissatisfied customer more quickly than your failure to deliver great customer service. On the other hand, providing great customer service makes everyone feel good. In the pre-digital era, a bad newspaper review was gone and forgotten in a few weeks. Today, on the internet, bad reviews live on virtually forever. Focus on providing great customer service. It will help to ensure that small issues don't blow up into massive and enduring marketing problems.

We had a site at which the property manager wanted to charge a resident for damaged flooring. The resident said it was damaged when he took possession and faulted the move-in checklist for failing to reflect the damage. It cost $250 to repair or replace the damaged flooring. The resident was so angry that he created a review website on which he posted hundreds of negative reviews using fake email accounts. He got on all the major online review sites and slammed the property and management.

Our solution was to settle with the former resident in exchange for his taking down all the negative reviews. It was frustrating, but this solution was better than suffering an endless series of blows to our leasing.

Check your reviews consistently. At least once a week, all reviews should be checked, and the need for responses should be addressed—both for positive and negative reviews. Most of all, make use of the reviews to help you identify and remedy problems. Here is an example:

Notice that the reviewer claims they could not get anyone to return a phone call. We began our response by emphasizing the positive aspects of the review and then by addressing the reviewer's complaint in a way that apologized and asked for a second chance to deliver the quality of service they deserved. Never express doubt about the sincerity of an unhappy customer. Instead, find a basis on which to build or rebuild a positive relationship. As for evaluating the complaint, we concluded that we had either a training issue or a people issue or both and that the issue indeed needed to be addressed and corrected.

The review was valuable because it alerted us to a problem. Look for a pattern. If you see several similar posts—in this case, complaints about unreturned calls—you know you have a genuine problem. If you see just one bad review or perhaps even a couple, it may just be that the leasing agent had a bad day. Nevertheless, the review should be brought to the attention of those staff members involved. It is important to ensure that your team is pleasant and professional to everyone they interact with, even crazy reviewers.

If you fix an issue a reviewer identified and the customer is now happy, it is important that you ask for the negative reviews to be removed.

Ask for positive reviews. This sounds so simple, but we often go for months without a leasing agent asking a happy resident to post a positive review on the web. When your team does something great for a customer *and they are telling you about it*, ask them to give you a positive review. Express your gratitude in advance. Most people are happy to post a positive review when asked. On the other hand, nobody needs to prompt an unhappy resident to post a review. They are self-motivated. Courtney hosts review competitions every few months to see which of her staff members can get the most reviews to mention them during a set period of time, and the winner usually receives a gift card. While you can't request a positive review, you can specifically make sure that you're requesting reviews from prospects or residents who are actively letting you know that they're having a positive experience. This is a great way to keep your ratings up and to help keep the negative reviews from being the main focal point when someone searches for your property.

Respond to negative reviews and remove fake negative reviews. Negative reviews fall into one of three buckets:

1. *Legitimately upset residents whom your team has let down in some way.* You cannot fix people, but you can and must fix problems. That is why you need to make someone on the team responsible for researching and checking this category of reviews. The property manager needs to make sure team members are working to fix legitimate issues quickly, so they will not happen again. But the very first priority is to respond to the resident who posted the review and to begin the process of making things right.

2. *Upset residents who owe money, have been evicted, and/or have broken a property rule.* Respond promptly—without, however, debating the merits of the issue. Courteously invite and advise these reviewers to discuss the issue with the property manager.

3. *Competitors.* Believe it or not, your competitors can—and sometimes do—post negative reviews on your site just to bring your rating down. Such tactics are not rampant, but we have seen it happen often enough to offer a word to the wise. Fortunately, it is easy to find out if a signed negative review is illegitimate. Look for the resident on your rent roll. If the reviewer is not found there, flag or dispute the review, explaining that the reviewer's name does not appear on any of your leases. Ask if the reviewer used a different name on the lease. If there is no response, get the negative review removed by flagging it

and asking others to flag it as well. Address all real concerns genuinely, sincerely, and vigorously. By the same token, act aggressively to purge all negative fake reviews. Monitor your reviews frequently!

The property reviewed here has a low rating, does not respond to reviews at all, has not been asking for current reviews, and has an unresolved management issue. Among the biggest problems is that this review is the first one that shows up when a prospective resident Googles its name. Remember, reviews should be monitored at least weekly.

How to counteract a bad review on Google

Let's detail the steps you can take to counteract a bad review on Google:

- Address legitimate issues promptly. Reach out to the reviewer. Work to make things right. Then ask the reviewer to remove the review.
- Even if you cannot make the customer happy, ask the reviewer to remove the Google review.
- If you believe you have addressed the reviewer's concerns, explain this in a response to the review.

- If you believe the review is unreasonable, unjustified, or simply fraudulent, flag and report the review to Google.
- In the meantime—whatever other actions you take—bury any negative review in positive reviews. Ask satisfied residents to post positive reviews. Do what you can to flood the Google Reviews site with positive reviews. You will increase your overall score and make the negative review far less impactful.
- If you have evidence that the negative review is factually untrue and malicious, pursue legal action to obtain a court order to have the review taken down. (However, never threaten the author of a bad review with a lawsuit. If you intend legal action, keep it to yourself and let your lawyer make the first move.)

How to flag a fake Google review

Fake Google reviews are not uncommon and require prompt and special treatment. Do not let them pass. Ignore them, and they will potentially live forever. Allowed to persist, they become indistinguishable from the truth.

Flagging a fake Google review is the first step toward motivating Google to remove false online reviews. Diligently examine Google's latest review policy statement to understand what is and is not deemed acceptable content in a review. For example, Google prohibits spam and fake content and requires a reviewer's content to reflect their genuine experience at a location or business. As currently constituted, Google policy also prohibits the following:

- Calls to action and offers of products and services
- Off-topic content
- Illegal, sexually explicit, and terroristic content
- Offensive and obscene language and gestures

- Dangerous and derogatory content
- Conflicts of interest
- Impersonation

When flagging reviews, there is a lot to be said for strength in numbers. That is, if you can recruit several users to flag the same review, the chances of Google removing the review are multiplied. But beware. Do *not* flag a review just because you disagree with it. Some complaints are subjective and genuinely matters of opinion. When you encounter these, respond as positively (and non-defensively) as you can. If you do not feel that the review merits a response, at least learn from it. Withhold criticism, and, whatever you do, don't whine.

This said, if the review is unwarranted, respond positively but firmly with a truthful counter-narrative. And if something does indeed seem fishy, go to Google's statement of policies and decide if the review violates any of them.

As a local business owner or company, you can flag reviews in two different ways. You may flag the review via Google Maps or by managing your Google My Business Reviews.

6: Evaluate Your Property's Website

Your website is critical. It offers to the public your location, floorplans, prices, contact information, and much more. Here is a checklist that can be used to monitor the success of your website.

Is Your Website Effective?

1. Does your website load fast on a desktop as well as on mobile browsers? Always test websites on the most common mobile browsers.

2. Have you tested your website? Use available online tools to test website download speed and other technical factors:
3. https://www.ionos.com/tools/website-checker   https://developers.google.com/speed/pagespeed/insights/
4. https://www.deadlinkchecker.com/website-dead-link-checker.asp
5. Is the website easy to navigate?
6. Are there grammatical errors or misspellings on your website?
7. Is the online application process easy to use?
8. Can residents pay on your website?
9. Can residents enter work orders easily through the website?
10. Are the phone number and other key contact information easy to locate?
11. Is the website optimized for the Google search engine?
12. Are property photos up-to-date and flattering?
13. Are amenities listed correctly?
14. Do you have a mapping location link on your site to help potential residents find you?
15. Are your square footages, floorplans, utilities, application fees, and so on presented correctly on the website?
16. Is your website competitive with your key competitors'? Don't guess. Go to your comps' websites. See how they are laid out and how they flow. Do you need to make changes?

Online Advertising

Advertising is meant to create a sense of urgency and get prospects to act. To ensure this happens, review online ads weekly. Confirm that the information provided in the ads is current and the phone numbers ring through to the property. Equally important is to make sure that all floorplans, square footages, utility services, and other details are accurate. Look at the photos in the advertising to ensure that they represent your product in the best and most realistic way possible.

Summary

Effective promotion begins with an effective marketing plan based on market research, a rational advertising plan, and messaging that is tailored to the key demographics relevant to your property. You need to formulate methods of reporting on all promotional and advertising channels so that you can analyze their effectiveness and make any necessary changes. You and your team need to adjust your marketing plan to address all changes in the marketplace on a regular basis. Make sure your marketing plan is working for you.

As in any competitive business, you must know what your competitors are doing. The easiest way to start is simply to ask them. Information gathered directly from the competition can be corroborated by online ads as well as secret shopping.

As you go about promoting your property, ensure that you understand the key difference between marketing and selling. *Marketing* is the process of getting consumers interested in whatever you are selling. *Sales* refers to all of the business activities you undertake that are intended to lead directly to the actual selling of goods and services. Marketing is an approach to a set of consumers. Selling is an approach to an individual prospect.

In advertising, it is essential to know—or discover—what tactics and strategies work and what do not. You need to supply clear, honest, and complete information. Understand that pictures are even more powerful than words when it comes to engaging a prospect. Invest in excellent photography.

These days a great website is essential for promoting a property. Create a website and then tear it apart—critically. Evaluate what works and what does not. Enhance the former and eliminate or fix the latter. Do the same for your online advertising. Advertisements that fail to create an *urgent* desire in your prospects to act could contribute negatively to your property's bottom line.

Make certain that all marketing and advertising presents an honest picture of who you are as a property and creates a sense of urgency to act. This is the key to success.

CHAPTER 5

The Fifth P Is for Process

We should work on our process, not the outcome of our processes.

—W. EDWARDS DEMING

To improve is to change; to be perfect is to change often.

—WINSTON CHURCHILL

People, price, product, and promotion are four of the key elements of property management. Each of these elements comes with its own requirements, opportunities, and problems. But all of these play a role in the fifth P, the *process*. People, Price, product, and promotion are essential to the process, with each impacting it differently.

In essence, every aspect of property management can be thought of as nothing more or less than people working on processes. The best companies in the world may or may not make the best products, but they have developed the best processes, which allow them to outperform their competitors. Consider the likes of Apple, Costco, and Amazon. These companies have the best processes in place and, as a result, are successful companies. Processes and greatness tend to go hand in hand. The processes that these companies have put in place are the reason they consistently outperform their competition.

PROCESS CHECKLIST

1. Can the property's processes be improved?
2. Are the major processes monitored regularly?
3. What expense controls are in place?
4. Is fraud a problem on the property?
5. Is the property being correctly and effectively maintained?
6. Are leasing processes efficient and effectively executed?

1: Can the Property's Processes Be Improved?

Just as you should continually audit and evaluate the other 4 P's, you should also take stock of all your major processes with the objective of improving them. This requires two management mindsets:

1. A conviction that your processes can use improvement.
2. The confidence that you and your team are capable of providing the necessary improvement.

How can you begin? Start by recalling that property management is, at the core, people working on processes. Capture the big picture that reveals how each process operates. Identify each major process, then sit down and sketch out a flowchart for each. If you need a motivating nudge to undertake this task, start with any business process that is causing you problems. Map out the process using a flowchart.

The more difficult it is to create the flowchart of a dysfunctional process, the more you need the flowchart to guide you to a fix. The act of creating a flowchart will force you to look at each step of what you are doing and consider if each step could be improved. You cannot improve a process without understanding all the steps involved. Assessing the performance of each of those steps, one by one, will help you understand.

Close the Gap

"The gap" is the difference between what senior management thinks or believes is happening and what is actually taking place at the property. Every business has the gap. Fortunately, following the 5 P's will help you begin to close the gap at your property.

As stated before, managing your property is nothing more than following specific processes. To help you improve the ones that need to be adjusted, you must first understand what each person's role is in those processes.

You are the manager, the regional manager, or the owner, right? Who should be more familiar with the processes? The people who are working every day with those processes. Ask people in different roles—property manager, leasing agent, maintenance supervisor, and so on to explain *their* processes to you. This will reveal each person's role in the overall process.

It is supremely important that you do not criticize, scold, or argue. You are gathering facts and putting together a picture of the property's processes. So for now, just listen and learn. You need to evaluate each critical process from the perspective of those most closely engaged in executing it.

Once you determine that a process needs improvement, add a level of clarity to your understanding by asking each person who interacts in the process to map out their steps by independently creating a flowchart. Anyone in an on-site leadership position should also create a flowchart of this process to understand how it may affect their job.

Compare and contrast the results you get from each. For example, based on the flowchart created by the property manager and the flowchart created by the assistant manager, you can readily determine if people are on the same page, working redundantly, or, even worse, working inefficiently.

Is the work of your staff coordinated and complementary?

For example, does the manager see the process the same way as the assistant manager? Performing the flowchart exercise will help you understand what does and does not need improvement so that everyone has the same goal in mind.

Are key processes put in writing and followed?

Don't assume they are. Just because month-end closeouts and turns are being done, it does not necessarily mean that they are being done correctly or efficiently.

> *If you can't describe what you are doing as a process, you don't know what you're doing.*
>
> —W. EDWARDS DEMING

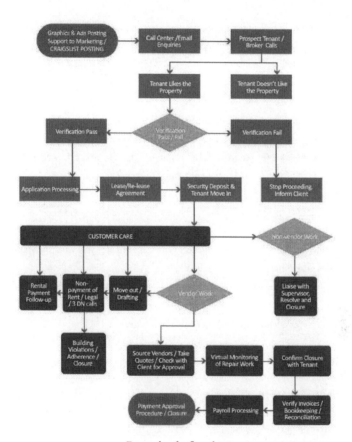

Example of a flowchart

After you have collected your flowcharts and examined them, talk to the senior team members at the property. Use their flowcharts as a basis for the conversation. When you see something on a chart that catches your eye, ask about it. Ask people how they do things. You may have suggestions for a better way, or you may find that the person on the ground has figured out a better way than yours.

Ken owned a small fifty-four-unit property in Atlanta in the late 1990s. He recalls walking into the leasing office and seeing the property manager adding up rental collections with a tape calculator so that she could put the totals on an Excel spreadsheet! She had no idea that the Excel spreadsheet had a sum calculator built into the program.

Now, her mistake was understandable since this was pretty early in the days of the PC and its applications, when we were all still in the process of changing from paper ledgers to computers. Ken certainly did not scold or berate her. Instead, he just showed her how the Excel sum calculator feature worked, and she immediately realized that using it would save her time and tedious effort. She did not feel that she had been put down but, quite the contrary, was grateful for having been given useful, time-saving information, which made her daily routine much easier. Little improvements in a process can pay big dividends in terms of efficiency, morale, and job satisfaction.

In analyzing the flowcharts, learn and help. Remember, the goal here is to improve each person's job function. Look for evidence of inefficiencies among the different functions and use the flowcharts to improve those processes. When a change is made to one process, make sure that it is beneficial to all employees and the property as a whole. Anytime you are trying to improve a component process, you should involve all employees who are impacted. This is a step toward optimizing all processes at the property.

The objective of "closing the gap" is to make the process easier and more efficient for all employees.

Change Is Constant

Read the trade magazines, go to trade shows, and speak to competitors. The property-management industry is changing very quickly. Your competitors may have processes that you may want to adopt. Keep an open mind. Always look for new and innovative ways to approach an inefficient process.

Not all that long ago, the lifeblood of the industry ran through paper apartment guides and magazines. These were the main venues for advertisements. Today, it's all online, and even that is evolving rapidly. Craigslist used to be the unquestioned king of advertising. Now it is Google Ads. Google Ads is the place to be and the top spot for leads. Change is constant.

> *If the rate of change on the outside exceeds the rate of change on the inside, the end is near.*
>
> —JACK WELCH

2: Are the Major Processes Monitored Regularly?

What processes should you check and how often? This section lists the processes to check. As for frequency, some items should be checked weekly, but everything should be checked, at a minimum, monthly. That is what the most successful companies do.

Processes to Check on a Regular and Ongoing Basis

1) Office

- Review bad debt.

- Review your screening process.
- Review your collection policies and how they are executed.
- Review move-outs and statements of deposit accounts.
- Inspect vacant units.
- Review expense controls that are in place.
- Review financial statements and check for fraud.

2) Maintenance

- Review work orders.
- Review rent-ready units.
- Review shop and inventory.

3) Leasing

- Review lease files.
- Review closing ratios and leasing process.

Office

Review bad debt

What do you do when you check the weekly report and see residents with unpaid rent? What is your process?

Bad debt is a fact of business life, but some of the causes of this problem are within your control while others, such as external economic conditions or events such as recession, major plant layoffs, or individual job loss, are not.

Review your screening process

Renting is a form of credit, and, like any business that extends credit, leasing calls for some prudent processes and standards to assess the

creditworthiness of a prospective resident. Review your screening process.

What are your minimum standards for leasing? Many properties
require the following:

a. Three times the rent in monthly income
b. One year of employment history
c. Minimum credit scores (varies throughout the industry)
d. Two years of acceptable rental payment history
e. No prior evictions on file
f. No major criminal records

These items should be standard in your process for leasing apartments. Making exceptions to them often creates problems. That said,
no manager likes to turn away a prospective resident. Your process
should include items to consider when deciding whether to make exceptions to your normal screening process. You may decide to accept
guarantors. If so, you should ensure their creditworthiness. Requiring
that a guarantor demonstrate an income that is five or six times the
rent is generally prudent.

If the leasing team makes an excessive number of overrides on
screening applications or if they accept applicants with faulty documentation, regard these as red flags which may be a   warning of
approaching bad-debt problems.

When Ken had a property with a bad-debt problem, he reviewed
all the screening criteria but could not find any red flags. So why were
there so many evictions? He dug deeper. Delving into the files, he discovered multiple instances of fraudulent proof of income. Several of
the residents had been providing false W2s and pay stubs, and even

false IDs. It is critically important to spot-check your files and supporting documentation on a regular basis. Learn to recognize the difference between authentic and bogus documentation.

Review your collection policies and how they are executed

Bad debts require collection, and every property needs to have effective, rational collection policies in place. Here are the questions you should ask:

- Are the same rules applied consistently to every resident?
- Are payment plans accepted?
- Are decisions on payment plans consistent?
- What is management's policy for such plans?
- Is management's policy adhered to?
- Does the management team make frequent or arbitrary exceptions?

Making exceptions to the rules of any process is inherently dangerous. Exceptions train residents to pay other debts first before paying the rent. Make sure your team is calling, emailing, and texting the delinquent resident as well as that resident's emergency contact. This should be done daily in an earnest effort to collect rental payments.

Is it proper to notify the emergency contact? Absolutely. *Not paying rent is an emergency!*

The more persistent and consistent the team is, the better chance you will have of collecting rent from your problem residents. "Persistent and consistent" does *not* give you a license for harassment, but the approach does ensure that evictions are filed on time, every time. If residents never see an eviction notice on their door, they will not fear being evicted. *Do not make exceptions.* Pay the costs to file the eviction and then charge the costs back to the resident as part of the late payment penalty.

Consistently review and complete the following:

- Ensure that the property team fills out a delinquency report every week.
- Require that the property team regularly update any collection efforts. This will enable management or owners to properly monitor the collection process.
- Spot-check the work being done by the property team by calling on some of the delinquent residents.
- Review the property's eviction records to ensure that the evictions are being made in a timely manner.
- Spot-check ledgers for partial payments.
- Examine the ledgers to spot any write-offs to existing residents.

All these are signals and possibly red flags. Individually, instances of laxity on the part of the property team may seem small, but they can become larger, even systemic problems if they are not consistently reviewed and addressed.

Example Bad Debt Report

Review third-party collections. After your on-site team has exhausted all attempts to collect on bad debt, your staff should involve a collection company. The on-site team should make every effort to collect all monies due, as collection companies generally do not have a great track record of successful recovery and have typically high commission percentages. Any old evictions or skips should be provided to the collection company monthly.

According to some studies, nationwide average recovery rates in the apartment industry are low, and, like all bad debt, rates decrease as accounts age. The Association of Credit and Collection Professionals (ACA International), the largest trade association representing the debt-collection industry, reported a 9.9 percent average recovery of consumer accounts by third-party debt-collection agencies in 2016. In short, only one out of every ten collection accounts are successfully recovered, and the odds diminish with age. Studies conducted by the ACA conclude that for every thirty days an account remains open and unworked, it is 16 percent less likely to be collected.

Waiting until an account is 90, 180, or 365 days in arrears before turning it over to an external agency sets you up for disappointing results. So it is important that files be given to a collection company as soon as your own efforts to collect have failed. Many management companies require staff to turn over all bad-debt files to a third-party collection company within 30 to 45 days of the default. Many of the current property-management software systems include a built-in bad-debt system, which makes it easier to transmit the files to a collection company. These may or may not be the best options for your company, so we urge you to do your research on various options before choosing.

Choosing a collection agency. It is no secret that debt collection has a mixed reputation at best—from the point of view of both creditors and consumers. You can search and compare companies locally or online. Look for a company that has both special expertise in collecting residential apartment bad debts and a reputation for good, ethical collections practices. Ask for referrals from trusted professionals in your network, such as your lawyer or accountant. Ensure that the agency you are considering is a member of ACA International, the Association of Credit and Collection Professionals, the leading trade organization for the industry. Here is what to look for in an agency:

- Ask how the agency tracks and finds debtors. Ask to see a sample report and how often they send those reports.
- The agency should report debts to Experian, Equifax, and TransUnion. This is one of the most persuasive collection tools agencies use to motivate a debtor to pay his or her debt.
- For local agencies, check the reviews on Google.
- Check the company's Better Business Bureau record and rating.
- The company should carry a minimum of $1 million dollars of liability insurance.
- Check to ensure the agency is authorized to collect in all fifty states. You want to make sure that if your resident moves, the agency will still be able to collect on the bad debt legally.

The Consumer Financial Protection Bureau administers the Fair Debt Collection Practices Act (FDCPA), and it takes complaints. You might be able to check on complaints against an agency you are considering.

- Ask for references from other landlords who use the prospective agency's services. References are important so that you may learn not only how well the agency collects your money but also how they treat their clients.
- What is the agency's commission rate? Rates generally range from 30 percent to 50 percent of the amount collected. You may find a company that charges on the low end of the scale, but such companies may have limited resources and not be successful at collecting your debt. Would you rather see a recovery of 70 percent of nothing or 50 percent of a $10,000 debt? A "bargain" commission rate could end up costing you more.

Violating consumer fair lending laws in an attempt to collect a debt can render that debt uncollectible and, worse, might result in a countersuit against the collector and *you*. According to the Consumer Financial Protection Bureau, a collection agency must not do any of the following:

- Call before 8 AM or after 9 PM
- Call at work
- Harass, oppress, or abuse someone
- Lie or make false statements
- Use unfair practices
- Conceal identity
- Disregard a written request to cease contact

Review move-outs and statements of deposit accounts

Are you losing money? Part of the problem may be in your process, and that means your property-management team is costing you money.

Consider damage charges, for instance. Does the property have an established, unambiguous, and reasonable list of damage charges? Many property-management software packages include standard move-out charges. This can be a great help, but you must ensure that the schedule of damages is up-to-date and customized to your area. Do you know how much it costs to replace a damaged carpet *in your market*? Is this reflected in the data input into your software? If you are charging to recoup replacement costs calculated for 2010 but it is 2023, you are likely losing money on every repair. Make certain that you are aware of the current replacement costs in your specific market.

When you decide to defer a delinquent account for collection, make certain all charges are accurately reflected on your charge list. The property's move-out process should include a file with a list detailing the charges, photos of the damages, and a letter explaining the charges in every file. This accounting process should be accurately completed and compiled before the resident's file is sent to collections.

Be transparent. "In my beginning is my end," the poet T. S. Eliot wrote. Much of property management focuses on beginnings and acquiring residents, but your process must incorporate endings as well, and it must do so from the very beginning.

Resident liabilities and responsibilities should be clearly spelled out in the leasing agreement and never buried in small print. In the real world, some residents violate their agreements and responsibilities. They break their promises. But also in the real world, some residents are just not fully aware of the agreement they made. You are not in the business of playing "gotcha." Maximizing residents' awareness of their rights, liabilities, and responsibilities benefits both you and the resident. Your process, therefore, should promote and maximize awareness.

As soon as a resident gives notice to vacate, transmit a letter of acknowledgment that prominently features move-out instructions. Do this immediately—which means well before the move-out day. Here is a sample:

RESIDENT MOVE-OUT INSTRUCTIONS

This office acknowledges receipt of your notice to vacate on _____

_____.

The following information is provided to assist you in your move-out and will aid in the expeditious return of your security deposit.
THE REQUIREMENTS TO BE FULFILLED ARE LISTED BELOW BUT ARE NOT LIMITED TO:

1. Full term of Lease Agreement.
2. A full _____ day's written notice has been given prior to vacating the apartment and submitted to the office where rent is paid. You will be charged for the fulfillment, even if you do not physically occupy the premises.
3. No unpaid charges or delinquent rents.
4. All keys returned.
5. Forwarding address left with manager.
6. When an apartment is vacated that has been occupied by a resident with a pet, a sanitation fee will automatically be deducted from the security deposit for the extermination of fleas and deodorizing of the apartment.

7. Transmitters, gate cards, parking sticker, garage door openers, etc. must be returned.
8. Schedule a walk-through.

A final inspection of the apartment will be made only after the resident has completely moved out. If the move-out is completed during regular business hours, a representative of the property will walk the apartment with the resident. If, after the move-out inspection, the apartment does not meet the prerequisites, charges will be made as shown on the accompanying list. The prices quoted are indicative of the approximate average charge per item described.

Security deposits will be returned by mail to the forwarding address left with the manager within the number of days required in the lease after the move-out inspection. Refunds cannot be picked up at the office.

Kitchen Cleaning	Bathroom Cleaning	Miscellaneous
Oven $30.00	Shower Doors $15.00	Window Coverings $50.00
Broiler Plan $10.00	Toilet(s) $10.00	Carpet Cleaning $35.00
Drip Pans $ 2.00	Tub $20.00	Carpet Repairs $100.00
Stove & Vent Hood $10.00	Sinks/Countertops $35.00	Trash Removal $60.00
Refrigerator/Freezer $40.00		Wallpaper Repair $150.00

Dishwasher $10.00		Painting $200.00
Cabinets/Countertops $30.00		Vinyl Floors $25.00
		Holes in Walls $75.00
		Carpet Not Vacuumed $20.00
		Patio Cleaning $15.00

REPLACEMENT CHARGES

If any items are missing or damaged to the point that they must be replaced when you move out, you will be charged for the current cost of the item, plus labor and service charges. An example list of replacement charges is provided below. **These are average prices. If the property incurs a higher cost for replacing an item, you will be responsible for paying the higher cost.**

Please note that this is not an all-inclusive list; you can be charged for the replacement of items that are not on the list.

Window glass $150	Fire extinguisher $ 35
Doors $100	Patio glass door $15
Light fixtures $ 50	Window screens $ 35
Ice trays $ 3	Light bulbs $ 1

Patio screens $100	Crisper cover $ 15
Countertops $250	Mailbox keys $ 25
Door keys $ 35	Woodwork $ 50
Disposal $ 65	Mirrors $ 60
Blinds $ 50	Refrigerator shelves $ 30
Carpet Actual cost	Cabinets Actual cost
Flooring Actual cost	
Wallpaper Actual cost	

_____ Management
_____ Resident(s)

Improve your net operating income (NOI) by physically spot-checking Statements of Deposit Accounting (SODAs). Ensure that all units about to be vacated are walked and examined with a critical eye. Check the reports. Are all damages being assessed correctly and charged appropriately?

The best way to ensure this evaluation process is being performed correctly and diligently is to walk move-outs with your team. How much did they actually charge for damages versus what should have been charged? Comparing the two charges is the best way to determine if the correct process is being followed. You will know immediately if retraining is necessary.

It is surprising how many assistant managers delegate move-out inspections and assessment of charges to the maintenance supervisor or a leasing agent. Neither of these positions includes training in evaluating damage, assessing costs, and following through with the outgoing resident. The loss to net operating income in this area can be substantial.

In addition to making certain that the correct amounts are charged, spot-checking total move-out charges can be highly revealing and consequential. Inspect some recently vacated units and determine what the management team has charged. Compare your inspection to their charges. Did they miss anything?

Missed charges are astoundingly common. In fact, it is downright surprising how often damages that should have been charged were not charged. Sometimes the property team doesn't charge for things they consider insignificant. Those charges add up! Quite often the property team fails to charge for cleaning, wall damage, and carpet damage.

It is important to compare the initial move-in condition sheet with the move-out condition sheet before you assess any damage. It is simply a matter of before and after. Be reasonable. Normal wear and tear and the actual time of occupancy should play a role in determining charges. Nothing will upset a resident more than being charged for damages that they noted on the move-in inspection/condition report.

Inspect vacant units

Monitoring the move-out is only one part of the turn process. Just because your records show a unit is vacant, don't make any assumptions about its status or its condition without inspecting it.

You should monitor rent rolls and availability reports during regular monthly visits to the property, but units reported as vacant should be personally examined. For one thing, they may not be truly vacant! Sometimes units that are reported as vacant are in fact occupied. This can be a sign of bad bookkeeping or, worse, criminal trespass or fraud.

The only way to know for certain that units are truly vacant is to walk them and verify. As a regional manager, it is recommended that you spot-check vacant units that have been reflected on the rent roll for more than thirty days.

Check any units marked as *down units*. This designation is common practice in property management. Units requiring more than $5,000 to get them move-in ready are marked as *down* until the site has the funds in the budget to perform the repairs necessary to make them rent ready.

Check the units that have been vacant the longest. Why have they been vacant for so long? What is needed to get them leased? Is a move-in special necessary to lease certain units?

The best practice is to walk each vacant unit every month. If it is not possible to walk every unit, spot-check thoroughly.

What to Look for in Vacant Units

- *Make certain the unnecessary power is turned to the off position.* Minimize all utility bills on vacant units. If you walk into a vacant unit that has the AC turned down to fifty degrees during the summer months or turned up to ninety degrees on winter days, correct the situation, but also find out why this costly negligence has occurred. Third-party vendors may have left HVAC systems like that for some time. If so, charge the vendor to recoup the excess utility cost. This will remind them to be certain that they leave a unit the way they found it. Vacant units should have the HVAC turned up or down seasonally to keep the power bill low. All appliances should be in the off position—except for the refrigerator (to prevent mold).

- *Check for leaks, mold, and other major issues in vacant units.* Walking vacant units is of critical importance and will help you locate substantial issues. One cold morning while walking vacant units, Ken heard the sound of running water. He suspected water had been left running in the bathroom, but when he looked in the bathroom, he was surprised to see that no water was on. Still hearing the water, he kept looking and discovered that a pipe in the unit above had burst. The closet wall was wet, and water was pouring into the crawlspace.
- *Walk vacant units monthly—at a minimum.*
- *Review the quality of rent-ready units.* Walking vacant units is a great opportunity to review the performance of the maintenance team. A checklist detailing the progress of vacant units should accompany you during the inspection. This checklist should show the progress of units—painting, cleaning, maintenance, and punch-out—toward being fully rent ready. Reviewing these units regularly will be a great indication of the rent-ready quality the property delivers. Making certain that rent-ready standards are set and met is important to the overall success of the community.

3: What Expense Controls Are in Place?

Management companies fall into two main groups with respect to expense control policy: companies that use purchase order systems and companies that do not. What is the expense-control policy and process of your management company?

A company with a properly designed purchase order system can accurately tell owners what has been spent on the site up to the moment they check. Those that do not have such a system—mainly the smaller companies—must wait until the bills come in before they know how much they spent. This is like writing checks without recording them in your register. Without proper record keeping (purchase orders), your bank balance is not an accurate indication of what is left to spend or what has been spent.

Clearly, we believe it is unwise *not* to use a good purchase order system. Before you engage a management company, ask about this. If a prospective company does not use a purchase order system, we suggest you keep shopping. These days, most property-management software includes purchase order functionality.

A good purchase order system helps you in several ways. It prevents duplicate or erroneous invoices from getting paid. It serves as a legal document in the event of a dispute with a vendor over payments. It allows you to track and control spending by letting you know exactly how much you have left in your budget for the current month. Finally, it provides an audit trail.

The PO (Purchase Order) Bomb

If you visit a site that has a history of expense overages, ask yourself the following questions:

- Is the office disorganized?
- Is there an expense or NOI (net operating income) bonus plan in place?
- Is the manager overwhelmed?

These are early warning signs that demand attention. They are the ingredients of a recipe for what we call the *PO bomb*. Invoices have been stuffed in drawers, and the PO bomb has just blasted your owner's bottom line!

Check the vendor statements. This will show which invoices have been issued and for how long as well as how much. The vendors who most commonly drop PO bombs are painters, cleaners, carpet cleaners, and smaller vendors. Why? The larger vendors are much more rigid in their processes, while many of the smaller vendors still use paper invoices, which are subject to manipulation by managers who want to push invoices to the next quarter, so that the property can get its performance bonus. Larger companies will typically not allow this to happen.

The only way to avoid PO bombs is to enforce a strong PO system and let vendors know that if they perform work or provide services or supplies without a PO, they will not be paid. All vendors should sign paperwork stating that payment is guaranteed only with a purchase order number issued by the property. This is a great tool to have in place when a vendor breaks the rules. In addition, all vendors should be required to send a copy of their aging delinquency statements to the corporate office for review.

Note, by the way, several vendors require that a PO be issued before any item or service is ordered. They have the right idea, as this also protects their best interests. In any case, it is critically important to ensure that the purchase order system is being used correctly and consistently. Employees should know that failure to adhere to the PO system is a breach of integrity and will not be tolerated.

Review Financial Statements and Check for Fraud

Reviewing financial statements every month is a critical responsibility of the property manager, the regional manager, and the asset manager. Your goals here are to drive revenue and reduce costs. As you review these statements, continually ask yourself what steps could have been taken and could now be taken to increase income or reduce costs.

If you are reviewing paper printouts, read them with your *red* felt pen in hand and use it to make notes. Why *red*? Because it stands out. If you are reviewing the statements onscreen, make liberal use of your software's comment feature. Be certain to call out every major item for review and red-flag each one.

Financial statements encompasses a range of documents. Which ones should you be reviewing every month, and what should you be looking for?

1. *Trailing 12-month income statement.* This report allows you to spot breaks or changes in the property's financial trend, either up or down. It also allows you to see seasonal changes in the property. Natural gas prices are much higher in the winter than in the summer months. On sites that have central boiler systems or where the property is paying for this cost, you should be alerted if a pattern reverses or spikes up or down. Ask why these changes are occurring.

2. *Budget comparison report.* This report is very useful, provided that the budgets are accurate. Many management companies require managers to fill out monthly reports explaining any variances of 5 percent or greater in line items or budget categories. This can be a helpful exercise because it requires the on-site team to pay careful attention to expenses. It alerts to changes in income that warrant investigation.

   A great example of such a change is a spike in water costs on the most recent statement. First step: Task the maintenance team to check the property for leaks. Evidence of leaks is sometimes discovered by reviewing statements from the water management company, but by the time the property receives a statement, reviews it, sends out maintenance, and a leak is discovered, thirty to forty-five wasteful days have passed. This can be a problem because another thirty to forty-five days of leaks may be reflected on the next statement. Better to look out for this by acting on the clues in the budget comparison report. The on-site response will be timelier. You should also consider doing what many properties do, which is to employ a service such as WaterSignal (https://www.watersignal.com/), which alerts you to spikes in water costs.

3. *Balance sheet.* The balance sheet is a veritable EKG of vital processes. It is important to look at the balance sheet as well as the budget comparison report.

Now, what should you look for on a property's balance sheet?

1. *Cash accounts*: Are there any unexplained changes in your checking account balances?
2. *Reserves*: Is your accounting team pulling down replacement reserves? Cash is your lifeblood.
3. *Security deposits*: Is your accounting team transferring forfeited security deposits to your operating account?
4. *Fixed assets*: Are items being posted to these accounts instead of to P&L accounts?
5. *Accounts receivable (AR) and accounts payable (AP)*: Are AR and AP being handled properly? Is there a failure to charge allowance for doubtful accounts with correct write-offs? Are payables being paid in a timely manner? These are *all* red flags indicating that income and expenses are being overstated or understated and a shortage of cash flow for investors is looming. ACTION IS REQUIRED.

4: Is Fraud a Problem on the Property?

The organization should remove easy opportunities to engage in self-interested behavior. As Charlie Munger, vice-chairman of Berkshire Hathaway, says:

> A very significant fraction of the people in the world will steal if (A) it's very easy to do and (B) there's practically no chance of being caught. And once they start stealing, the consistency principle—which is a big part of human psychology—will combine with operant conditioning to make stealing habitual. So, if you run a business where it's easy to steal because of your methods, you're working a great moral injury on the people who work for you . . . It's very, very important to create human systems that are hard to cheat. A system is perverse when good people go bad because of the way the system is structured. If you run a big chain of stores and you make it easy to steal by your own sloppiness, you will cause a lot of good people to go bad. You will have created an irresponsible system.

As with many facts of life, no one likes to talk about fraud or think about it. But if you own or manage a few properties, ongoing fraud is not only possible, but also it is likely—highly likely. Only a small fraction of people commit fraud, but the reality is that fraud happens and you should expect it. Fraudulent activities generally originate from two major sources: employees and vendors.

Employee Fraud

Property management offers at least eight varieties of employee fraud:

1. **Check Games:** The employee deposits a rental check into his or her own account. This is done by altering a check or money order. Some employees even open a separate business account in the name of X Apartments and deposit rental checks into this account. Such fraud is usually committed on properties with high amounts of bad debt or rental concessions.

2. **Blank money orders:** This fraud occurs at properties with a substantial number of older residents and/or residents who are not fluent in English. Among both categories of residents, it is not uncommon for employees to offer their "assistance" by filling out money orders for the resident. Your rent collection process should include a strict policy barring employees from filling out money orders for residents.

3. **Accepting cash:** There is no legitimate reason for an employee to accept cash from a resident. Most management companies and properties have strict policies barring employees from soliciting or accepting cash. Violation of the policy is generally considered a cause for termination. Know the policy governing this in your company.

4. **Renting "vacant" units:** This happens when an employee leases units marked as *down* or *vacant* and pockets the income. We wish we could tell you that this is so far beyond the pale that it rarely happens, but outlandish as it may seem, it does happen and has happened to us. This is another reason to personally walk and spot-check all units marked as *down* or *vacant* to confirm that they are, in fact, unoccupied. If the staff

knows you regularly check vacant units, they are far less likely to attempt to pocket rental income for these spaces.

5. **Referral fee scam:** One of our sites showed a historic spike in referral fees, which are, of course, a legitimate promotional incentive. But we could see no legitimate reason for the magnitude of the spike, so we asked questions and soon sent an auditor to the site. She spoke to the residents involved, whose stories did not corroborate with the files. We investigated and discovered that the leasing agent was making up names and then splitting the referral fees with residents who were also involved. The lesson here? Ensure that you have a strong policy and procedure regarding referral fees.

6. **Inventory/supplies theft:** Purchase order systems should be in place and used for all expenses. Operating a business on the side is not fraudulent, but allowing the property to pay for your supplies is. Your company should have PO logs and require that all invoices include the unit number, reflecting the upgraded/replaced capital item that was purchased for that unit. The act of recording these items is a great deterrent against inventory and supply theft.

7. **Supply theft** is somewhat harder to prevent or deter than theft of capital items. Be vigilant, because parts, consumables, and other supplies that are frequently used in an individual's side business can easily be pilfered from the office or maintenance shop. A quarterly supply audit of both locations is advised. HVAC refrigerants and other miscellaneous items are regularly stolen. Audits are the most effective way to detect and discourage stolen supplies.

8. **Personal expenses on company accounts.** Watch invoices and receipts for personal items. One day, Ken was reviewing

Home Depot receipts and noticed several power tools purchased at the site. He asked about these, inspected the shop, and discovered that these tools were purchased by the maintenance supervisor for his personal use. The best defense against this kind of fraud is to spot-check invoices and ask questions.

9. **Kickbacks.** Ensure that your bidding process is documented and that you are aware of any friend or family relationships between employees and vendors. Check your pricing for commonly used items, and make sure they are in line. In other words, trust but verify.

Vendor Fraud

The most common forms of vendor fraud include the following:

1. **Measurement games (aka long/short yarding):** This is a scheme in which the vendor tells you it will take one thousand bales of pine straw and charges you for it but uses eight hundred bales. Another favorite is one used by flooring companies. They tell you a unit requires x yards of flooring and then install much less, thereby improving their profits.

2. Most of these frauds cannot be detected by simply eyeballing the results. Require your vendors to list out their measurements and compare not just their total bottom-line charges but how much material they intend to use. Getting multiple bids and measurements for comparison is recommended.

3. **Quality tricks:** Vendors may try to increase their profits at the cost of the property by quoting prices for a particular brand only to use an inferior (and cheaper) brand. Painters may accurately tell you it will take x gallons of paint for a job and then

water down the paint. Check their work to ensure that vendors are using the specified product and doing the work as stated.

4. **Scope change:** Some vendors bid on a job, stating that the project will require more work than necessary, or they will bid as necessary but only perform part of what is needed. For instance, if a vendor proposes to wrap windows and install siding over the wrap, you likely will assume that they did the job exactly as it was bid. However, the only way to be sure they are doing jobs as it was proposed is to inspect the work. Inspect what you expect.

5. **Billing for items not shipped or services not provided:** This happens quite often. Make certain that you get all the supplies and services you pay for.

6. **Vendors overcharging:** Always make sure your managers solicit and receive multiple bids. Check to ensure that your expenses at one property are in line with those of other properties in your portfolio. If, for instance, you notice a property paying $780 for painting a one-bedroom, whereas your other properties pay $300, you need to identify the cause of the price difference.

7. **Poor workmanship:** Some vendors will do work incorrectly to save time and money. Specifically, *their* time and money—on your dime. Your company ends up paying the costs for incorrectly performed work. Painting handrails that have been inadequately prepped saves the painter prep time, but the paint will never adhere properly and will likely chip and peel. It is critical that you and your team check the contractor's work to ensure the work is being performed correctly. If you are unfamiliar with the work and what is correct, Google the

applicable topic. You will almost certainly find informative videos that will help you better understand what you should inspect on various jobs.

5: Is the Property Being Correctly and Effectively Maintained?

Remember, it is far cheaper to retain an existing resident than it is to lease to a new one. Key to retention is top-notch maintenance, so it pays—literally pays—to ensure that your maintenance team is giving great service on all work orders. The following steps will help to create an efficient maintenance process.

Review Work Orders

1. Are work orders being filled out correctly? Many of the current property-management software platforms allow residents to fill out work orders online. It is important to make sure that correct information is being given to the maintenance staff. Telling a maintenance tech there is a leak in unit 2A does not allow him to come prepared to fix the issue. If instead the work order states there is a leak under the upstairs bathroom sink in unit 2A, the technician can come prepared to resolve the problem.

2. Are work orders being completed in a timely manner? If your team is taking forty-eight hours or longer to respond to work orders, you have maintenance issues. Some work orders require immediate responses. These priority issues include water leaks, plumbing backups, roof leaks, mold hazards, and fire hazards. Life safety issues should be addressed as soon as you

are notified or they are input into the online platform. Most management companies have an after-hours program to handle these types of calls that cannot wait until the next business day.

3. Resident callbacks on old work orders could be a sign that your team needs additional training or is not giving proper service. Check to ensure that callbacks are the exception rather than the rule on your properties.

4. Look for any recurring work orders that could be prevented. Examples of this are roof leaks/repairs and sewage backups. Do not pay more in roof repairs than it would cost to replace the roof, and do not respond to sewage backups over and over again. It may be time to jet or repair the line so that these backups do not reoccur. Nothing upsets a resident quite like a sewage backup into their unit.

5. Examine the use of outside contractors. As you review work orders, look for a pattern in the property that calls contractors to repair or replace items that could be repaired by the maintenance team. This is common after a large renovation. Instead of replacing or repairing items, the maintenance team becomes accustomed to calling contractors. This happens quite often in the case of HVAC contractors. Unnecessarily calling an outside contractor dings the owner's bottom-line profits and should be avoided.

6. Evaluate work order productivity. As you review work orders, ask yourself who is doing the work. For example, some maintenance supervisors would rather supervise than work. Is your maintenance supervisor a "working supervisor"? Find out who is actually fulfilling work orders. Ask questions.

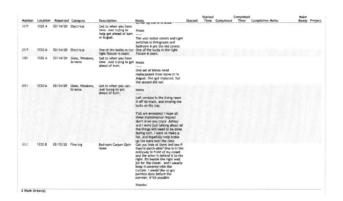

Example of a work order report from ResMan Software

Review Rent-Ready Units

It is important to inspect units designated *rent ready* and ensure that the posted status and reality coincide. While this topic was discussed briefly in chapter 3, *product*, we will go into more detail here. What should you check for in a rent-ready unit?

1. **Cleanliness.** Nothing will turn off prospective renters faster than a dirty unit. Check the appliances, especially the stove and oven. Check the drawers and shelves in the kitchens, bedrooms, and bathrooms, and look under the sinks.

2. **Smell.** Units should have a pleasant and clean smell. If there is a bad smell in the unit from cigarette smoke, pets, or constant cooking with oil or spices, an ozone treatment may be called for.

3. **Appliances and lighting.** All appliances should be checked and confirmed to be in working order. Lighting should be checked, and bulbs should be replaced as needed.

4. **Flooring.** Damaged or stained flooring should be repaired or replaced.

5. **Insects.** No bugs should be in the units.

6. **Overspray.** Look for overspray left by painters. It is not only unsightly, but it also gives residents the impression of careless workmanship, perhaps implying shoddy construction, and further conveys the sense that management does not care much about delivering a high-quality experience. Professional painters should not create overspray and, when it happens, should clean it up. Overspray is found most frequently on flooring, light fixtures, sprinkler heads, doors, cabinets, and countertops. This indicates a quality-control issue on the vendor's part and can cause major problems for you if it is not addressed. Indeed, your first problem may well be a prospective resident who, turned off, turns to your competition.

Verifying all these items should mean that the unit is truly rent ready. Everything should be in working order in a rent-ready unit. It is beyond frustrating for a new resident to move into a unit and discover a light bulb is out or the kitchen drawer falls out when you open it.

Review Shop and Inventory

While most of your maintenance process review should focus on results, you should also visit the maintenance shop during a property visit.

1. Is the shop clean and organized? An untidy and disorganized shop costs your maintenance team time and, therefore, costs

you money. The reason to keep a shop organized is to make it quick and easy to locate necessary tools and supplies.

2. Are HVAC logs filled out properly and updated? It is very important to make sure these forms are updated and filled out correctly. The fine for releasing refrigerant into the atmosphere can be up to $27,500 per day, per violation. It is important for the protection of the maintenance team and the management company that these logs are kept current and used consistently.

3. With respect to supplies and inventory, does the site have the most commonly used parts and supplies, and are these clearly labeled? Do you notice more than an average number of appliances sitting around in boxes? Most sites keep a hot water tank, an HVAC unit, and key parts on-site for emergency work orders. Anything beyond this should be questioned. In fact, question anything that provokes your suspicion. Ken once visited a shop and noticed some very nice lighting fixtures sitting in the boxes at the back of the shop. He knew that they did not use that brand on this site. He asked the supervisor and manager about the lights and, receiving no satisfactory answer, investigated. The supervisor had ordered them for installation in his home. If you don't ask, you will not know.

4. Are the tools on site the property of the company, or are they personal? When a property changes maintenance supervisors, it is recommended that a *take-over log* be reviewed, signed, and dated to document the transfer of expensive tools and equipment owned by the property. If these items are lost or stolen, the supervisor is responsible for replacing them. Inventories should be performed regularly at the site, and they should account for every item in the maintenance shop.

5. Are hazardous chemicals stored in proper fireproof containers? Glance around and make sure that flammable materials are safely and properly stored.

6: Are Leasing Processes Efficient and Effectively Executed?

Lease files are a critical part of the leasing process. Check them periodically. Just as it is important to maintain a well-organized office, lease files should also be organized, consistent, accurate, and up-to-date.

Review Lease Files

Use a standard checklist to ensure that all lease files are accurate and have been reviewed by the assistant manager and spot-checked by the property manager before they are finalized. Here is an example of a New Lease File Checklist. Note that leasing processes continue to change as more of the lease paperwork goes online.

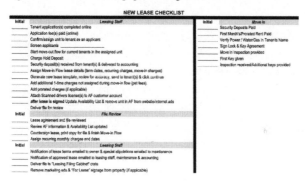

The items checked on a lease file audit can change according to the class of the property. Whether it is a conventional, section 8, or student-housing property may dictate items that require checking. However, here are key items that should be spot-checked on every lease file:

1. **Income verification.** Does the resident make enough money? Do they have the proper paperwork to support their reported income? Bad debt problems typically start with credit standards being lowered.

2. **Credit and background checks.** Ensure that background checks are in the files. Today, most background screenings are pass or fail. Make sure the credit checks are in the correct file.

3. **Signatures.** Are all lease agreements and lease addendums signed either physically or electronically? Ensure that all required forms are signed.

4. **Move-in condition inspection checklist.** Does the lease file contain a signed copy of the move-in condition checklist? This form must be completed, signed, and dated on the move-in date. Otherwise, if damages exist at move-out that were not present at move-in, it will be hard to win any damage reimbursement in court. Consider this a critical document.

5. **EPA lead-based paint addendum.** If your property was built before 1978, it is critical that lease files include a lead-based paint addendum. If this addendum is required and it is not in the files, the EPA (Environmental Protection Agency) has the authority to fine the property. EPA audit fines can add up quickly.

One of our property managers created "dummy files" with all the necessary forms in the proper order and placed them in a drawer in each leasing consultant's desk. This was a great tool for the leasing consultants, as they had at hand a correct file to check against theirs so they could be sure they had included the proper and accurate forms.

Review Closing Ratios and Leasing Process

Since leasing and renewals create almost 100 percent of your property's revenue, it is critically important that the process works smoothly and without error. Many of the current software platforms include integrated leasing workflows. Leads, tours, follow-ups, and the signing of leases and move-ins are all accounted for on one platform. This makes it easier for the leasing agents to track and follow up on leases and renewals.

The most crucial elements to note in your review of a property's leasing process are as follows:

1. **The presence of active tracking and updates.** For properties that show critically slow leasing, a requirement that property managers and/or leasing managers send the regional manager and company headquarters (or the owner) weekly or even daily leasing updates is highly beneficial. The mere act of asking and reviewing the leasing effort will tend to increase these efforts. You don't need a long, complex report, just a simple document reflecting the summary of efforts and results for that time period.

2. **Closing ratios.** We know that a closing ratio should be calculated by dividing the total number of actual applications by the total number of leads. So, if a leasing agent gets one hundred leads and closes twenty-five applications, they have a 25 percent closing ratio. Most leasing agents should have a closing ratio between 20 percent and 30 percent. It is possible that

some might be higher, but beware of outlier patterns. Focusing on statistics sometimes results in manipulation. The most common manipulation is to remove true leads. Placing true leads in a non-traffic category will decrease the divisor and make the closing ratio look better than it is. Sometimes leasing agents will cherry-pick leads to improve their leasing numbers as well. A 70 percent closing ratio over a period of six months should be a red flag that something is wrong with the reporting process.

3. **Improve leasing agent closing ratios.** Team-building culture, training, and incentives can have a huge impact on improving closing ratios. The most common mistake is that leasing agents simply fail to follow up on leads. Courtney often refers to herself as a "nosy manager" because she frequently digs into her staff's prospect communications to review their follow-up techniques and timelines. Follow-up should be immediate if the prospect is actively inquiring, and every two days if they've stopped responding, until they either unsubscribe or tell you they're no longer interested.

4. **Listen to leasing phone calls.** Software programs record calls to the property, so you have available to you a record of leasing calls. Monitoring or reviewing these calls is a great tool for training and quality assurance purposes. Consider the following:

   - How are the phones being answered?
   - Is contact information being gathered?
   - Are resident and prospect names being used when they call?
   - Does the agent seem inviting and friendly?

The best leasing agents are almost always smiling while they speak to prospects. Smiles are audible on a phone call.

Remember: the goal of any leasing call is a call to action. The goal of the call is to get the prospect to the property. Make the appointment, get follow-up information, and call to verify the appointment time, if necessary.

Alert the on-site leasing team that you regularly review their recorded calls. The mere act of reviewing the calls reinforces the importance of critical leasing skills and the role they play in the overall success of the property.

5. **Formulate action plans for improving leasing agents.** Almost every property has a leasing agent who needs to improve their leasing and closing skills. Ensure that the property-management team has in place a formal and informal training plan for leasing agents. The formal process should be laid out in writing. This plan should include the following:
   - Role playing of phone calls and site tours
   - Reading of leasing and sales books
   - Online courses
   - Classes dedicated to leasing

The informal process should allow the leasing agent to see and hear how other agents handle objections, how they schedule appointments, how they close prospects, and so on.

Summary

Property management consists simply of people working through processes. All good companies make good products, but the companies that outperform the others have the best processes in place. They allow them to consistently outperform their competition.

Develop two mindsets—a conviction that your processes can be improved, and the confidence that you and your team are capable of improving them. This chapter has given you the tools to assess your processes and improve them. It is aimed at closing the reality gap between what you, as a member of senior management, believe is happening and what is actually taking place at the property. The objective is to make improvements in specific processes that impact the collective process in the operation of the property. Know how each of the processes on your property contributes to or subtracts from revenue. Then solve your process problems and continuously monitor those solutions.

CHAPTER 6

Checklists

> *Checklists turn out . . . to be among the basic tools of the quality and productivity revolution in aviation, engineering, construction—in virtually every field combining high risk and complexity. Checklists seem lowly and simplistic, but they help fill in for the gaps in our brains and between our brains.*
>
> —ATUL GAWANDE, *surgeon and author of The Checklist Manifesto: How to Get Things Right*

In this final chapter, you will find, all in one place, the major checklists used in the preceding five chapters. As we have learned, the checklist is not only the key to good management but also plays an important role in just about any relatively complex endeavor people undertake.

The Surprising Power of a Checklist

"No wise pilot, no matter how great his talent and experience, fails to use his checklist," Warren Buffett's Berkshire Hathaway partner Charlie Munger declared. Commercial air travel is so safe that if you flew every day of your life on a commercial airliner, you could expect to suffer a fatal accident after nineteen thousand years of the 365/7 flying routine.[1]

What makes this so?

The two-person flight deck crew systematically runs down an exhaustive safety checklist before the aircraft even begins to taxi out to the runway. And if something does go wrong in flight, there is, at the crew's fingertips, a how-to checklist for virtually every conceivable situation.

So where does the surprising power of a checklist come from?

The philosopher Plato bewailed the invention of writing. He said it discouraged people from fully developing their faculty of memory because they could always just write things down. Plato predicted that, in the fullness of time, the human memory would atrophy. In contrast, the ancient Chinese were far more appreciative of writing, as this proverb suggests: "The faintest ink is more powerful than the strongest memory."

A checklist aids, augments, and extends human memory. In *The Checklist Manifesto*, the American surgeon Atul Gawande relates what happened in a San Francisco ER when a man was brought in with an abdominal stab wound. The patient was about to be taken to surgery to assess the level of damage, which, based on the man's behavior and vital signs, did not seem severe.

Then, without warning, he crashed and had to be rushed into the OR. Once the surgeons began to cut, they discovered that what had appeared to be a relatively minor wound was, in fact, life-threatening.

---

[1] Anxieties.com, "How Safe Is Commercial Flight?"
https://anxieties.com/86/flying-
howsafe#:~:text=You%20are%20nineteen%20times%20safer,die%20than%20in%2
0your%20car.&text=If%20you%20are%20going%20to,than%20on%20a%20comm
ercial%20jet.

How could the doctors in the ER have so seriously misjudged the problem? Gawande explains:

> There are a thousand ways that things can go wrong when you've got a patient with a stab wound. But everyone involved got almost every step right—the head-to-toe examination, the careful tracking of the patient's blood pressure and pulse and rate of breathing, the monitoring of his consciousness, the fluids run in by IV, the call to the blood bank to have blood ready, the placement of a urinary catheter to make sure his urine was running clear, everything.

What had the medics missed, and why? "No one remembered to ask the patient or the emergency medical technicians what . . . weapon . . . made the wound." It turned out, it was a military bayonet! As one doctor remarked, "Your mind doesn't think of a bayonet in San Francisco." This vicious weapon had penetrated the overweight victim more than a foot deep, nicking the aortic artery in addition to doing other grave damage.[2]

That doctor was right: you *don't* think of a bayonet assault in San Francisco. The medical personnel thought of all the usual things without resorting to any checklist, but it turns out that a checklist was precisely what they needed: something to tell them to do A, B, C, and D as well as E: *Ask what object or weapon caused the injury.*

The patient survived, but it was the closest of close calls.

Gawande recalls having read an essay by two philosophers, Samuel Gorovitz and Alasdair MacIntyre, when he was training as a surgeon.

---

[2] Atul Gawande, *The Checklist Manifesto: How to Get Things Right* (New York: Picador, 2010), 3.

The subject of the essay was the nature of human fallibility, and the two philosophers argued for the existence of "necessary fallibility," which makes some things we want to do beyond our capacity to do them for the simple reason that we are neither omniscient nor all-powerful. Sometimes and in some situations, control is not within our reach.

The two components of this "necessary fallibility" are ignorance and ineptitude.

Ignorance. We may simply have insufficient knowledge or training. Say the faucet in a kitchen sink in one of your units sprung a leak where the water inlet hooks up to the faucet. "Hey," the maintenance tech protests, "nobody told me I was supposed to use plumber's tape on the connection between the supply and the faucet!"

The answer to ignorance is training and experience and making certain the property manager hires maintenance personnel with both.

But what about *ineptitude*?

Sometimes, the knowledge exists, but it is not applied correctly. "Hey, I used plumber's tape!" But did you use enough? Did you wind it around the screw threads correctly? Did it stay flat, or did it twist up like a piece of used chewing gum?

In December 1998, NASA launched the Mars Climate Orbiter, a $125 million space probe designed to study the Martian climate. The probe weighed 745 pounds, but measureless tons of knowledge had gone into designing, building, launching, navigating, and controlling it.

Well, the Jet Propulsion Laboratory used the metric system of meters and millimeters in its careful calculations, whereas the builders of the craft, Lockheed Martin Astronautics, used the English system of inches and feet. The result was a faulty application of knowledge, as acceleration readings measured in *English* units were misapplied to a *metric* measure of force. The Orbiter missed Mars entirely and was quite literally lost in space. With that loss came a loss to both science and the taxpayer. A checklist that included making sure everyone was using the same system of measurement would have benefitted both science and the Treasury.[3] Ignorance? Not here. Ineptitude then? More than likely, yes.

Managing a rental property is not as delicate a proposition as surgery or as complex a project as sending a spacecraft to a distant planet and landing it safely there. But it does involve a set of dynamic relationships among buildings, technologies, finances, and human beings, which means that a lot can go wrong because of ignorance and, even more likely, ineptitude.

The upside here, however, is that property management is not a novel field of human endeavor, let alone a venture into an unknown region. A lot of people and companies manage properties, and a big bundle of best practices has been accumulated. Through training and experience, this body of knowledge can be learned.

But how can you make certain that the on-site staff *applies* it properly? For one thing, you never allow the staff to rely on memory. Instead, you give them checklists.

Let us admit that we ourselves are guilty. We have all done it. We are busy, and we visit a site, check in with the manager, speak to the team, walk the property, and leave the site only to remember, *way* down the road, two or three other things we should have checked. Maybe you leave these for next month. Chances are that the omission will create no great disaster. But who knows how many small ones?

---

[3] Ajay Harish, "When NASA Lost a Spacecraft Due to a Metric Math Mistake," *SimScale Blog* (January 26, 2021), https://www.simscale.com/blog/2017/12/nasa-mars-climate-orbiter-metric/.

Making use of the simple but comprehensive 5 P's checklists in this book will help—okay, *force*—you to remember all the things you should be asking.

There are certain things every property manager and management company *should* be monitoring and inspecting, and we have included many of them in this book. But it is also true that every management company has its own roster of metrics to monitor during on-site inspections.

While each management company or ownership group has certain key metrics and policies that they require their site employees to track, there are more similarities than differences from site to site and company to company. We have worked with more than fifteen third-party management companies over the years, and we can assure you that they are all looking at similar things on their sites. We have also heard our share of property managers complain about the number of forms and the "mountains" of paperwork with which the corporate office burdens them. (We ourselves have been guilty of some grumbling.) But the paper avalanche is diminishing in our world of real-time information. These days, we can use real-time online dashboards to view things like the number of leases, renewals, total collections, work orders, and on and on. All this data once had to be manually entered into weekly reports for owners and senior managers. Now that we can pull this info and even see chat messages and emails, we don't necessarily need more data. What we need—and desperately—is more insight.

As Atul Gawande might tell us, *ignorance* is no longer the big problem in property management, but *ineptitude* often is. The 5 P's and their attendant checklists will keep you focused on the most important parts of our business.

The 5 P's Checklist

Date of Inspection: Property Inspected:

People

1. How does the team interact?
2. Is the site fully and adequately staffed?
3. Does the site have any scheduling issues?
4. Are there any performance or personality conflicts on the current team?
5. What team-building events are in place?
6. What are the training plans for the team(s)?
7. Are current performance improvement plans in place and effective?
8. Is communication clear, open, interactive, and effective on every level?

Pricing

1. Have you reviewed your property's pricing matrix?
2. Have you reviewed other income?
3. Have you reviewed the competitive market surveys?
4. Have you reviewed and adjusted specials and renewals accordingly?

Product

1. Does the property's curb appeal make a great first impression?
2. Are the property and amenities clean?
3. Is each model/unit clean and working properly?
4. Does the property play to its strengths?

Promotion

1. Review current marketing plan.
2. Review lead tracking software.

- Check closing ratios.
- Check follow-ups.
- Check inactive calls.
- Listen to sample leasing calls.
- Compare leads.

3. What is the competition doing?
4. Review paid ad programs.
5. Check Google reviews and other sites.
6. Evaluate your property's website.

Process

1. Can the property's processes be improved?
2. Are the major processes monitored regularly?
3. What expense controls are in place?
4. Is fraud a problem on the property?
5. Is the property being correctly and effectively maintained?
6. Are leasing processes efficient and effectively executed?

CONCLUSION

Assuming you have gotten this far because you have read this book—and that's a big assumption, because so many of us are in the habit of starting a book by skipping to the end—think about why you read it.

We can tell you the real reason we *wrote* it.

It is because managing property is managing lives. Shelter is up there with food, water, and clothing as one of the most basic of basic human needs. Ours is the business of providing for an essential need. Success in this business is all about how you provide for this need in ways that go far beyond the basics to make your property a community in which people want to live. Creating such a place, marketing it, sustaining it, delivering value through it, and reaping value from it in return, calls for a combination of imagination and bedrock good sense.

Differentiating your property from your competitors' means thinking outside of the box. What can you do and what can you provide to give your property an edge over the competition?

But before you can think *outside* the box, you must thoroughly and effectively think and function *inside* the box. Henry Ford's first Model T rolled off the assembly line in 1908. It was a remarkable car, practical, reliable, and affordable. But nobody can deny that cars have come a long way since, with innovations Ford could not have even dimly glimpsed. Yet today's "computers on wheels," as we sometimes call our cars, are still motorized transportation on four wheels, just like the 1908 Model T. That fact is the box whose details must be mastered before any contemporary carmaker can even begin thinking outside it.

We wrote this book to aid and accelerate thinking inside the box of property management. Because property management is about managing lives—those of your residents and your employees as well the life of your high-stakes business and investment—it has a multitude of moving (and breathing!) parts. All too easily, it can get out of hand. If you feel that happening to you, just pick up this book—again—and remember: the difference between chaos and control is the presence of processes and procedures. In effective property management, the first step toward creating processes and procedures is understanding the dimensions inside the property-management box. They are defined by the 5 P's: *people, pricing, product, promotion*, and *process.*

Effectively managing any residential property requires effectively managing each one of these 5 P's. By accepting this principle, this truth, those in executive leadership and owners of residential properties arm themselves with the knowledge of what to look for when they check, inspect, or audit any property. Knowing the 5 P's is the first step to identifying problems in need of solutions and opportunities waiting for realization. The checklists we have created for each P enable you to dig down into each and take their performance temperature. Turn to them whenever you visit or inspect a property. They will save you time and help ensure that you miss nothing important.

•

Do we believe this book is the Bible of property management? No. Nor was it meant to be. It is our hope that it will serve as a guide, an instrument, a tool, a time saver. We recommend that you have it handy whenever you inspect a property. It will substantially improve your odds of recognizing and flagging problems as well as opportunities when you make a property visit, and it will point the way toward improvement. It will almost certainly save you money, and it will very likely make you money. Chances are good that it will help your managers and other employees to be their best—even if, in some cases, that "best" turns out to lie outside of property management. Perhaps most important of all, this book may point the way to creating a better experience for your residents.

No, this is not the sacred book of property management. So use it for what it is: a frank, practical, and pragmatic guide to the property-management box—how to think inside it and how, where necessary or desirable, to think outside it.

THE AUTHORS

Ken Doble is the cofounder and CEO of QR Capital, an Atlanta-based real estate investment and operating company specializing in multifamily and student housing properties. Ken began more than two decades in real estate as the on-site property manager of a twenty-four-unit apartment community in Atlanta. He rose rapidly in the industry and, before cofounding QR Capital, was COO of an Atlanta-based multifamily developer, overseeing the firm's entire apartment and condominium unit portfolio, more than twenty-two thousand units in eleven states with an aggregate value of over $2 billion. He led each of the firm's major operational, investment, and reporting groups, including its property management, renovation, investment underwriting, human resources, and internal audit teams. A hands-on expert, Ken developed proprietary underwriting and rent optimization software, as well as innovative cost- and expense-control systems and procurement protocols for use in multifamily property underwriting and operations.

Before entering the world of real estate, Ken Doble was a US Army paratrooper who saw combat in Panama and the Persian Gulf War.

Courtney Winters is a regional manager for a student-housing management company based out of West Lafayette, Indiana. A University of Tennessee graduate, she started in the industry at one of Ken's Knoxville, TN, properties as a leasing manager in 2015, and she has since progressed through every on-site management position at multiple properties prior to moving to the corporate level in 2022.

Throughout her time, she has managed a team responsible for annually leasing and maintaining upwards of seven hundred accounts, and she currently has over 1,300 beds in her portfolio and growing. She has been an NAA CAM certification holder since 2019.

Courtney also proudly welcomed her son, Quintin, into the world in 2022 while in the process of working on this book.

Made in the USA
Columbia, SC
30 November 2024

47967851R00098